Pelican Books
The Origins of Modern Leftism

Richard Gombin, who is French, was
attached to the Centre national de la
recherche scientifique when he wrote
this book. He has already published
two books, *Le Projet révolutionnaire*
(*The Revolutionary Project*), and
Les Socialistes et la guerre (*Socialists
and War*), and has worked in
collaboration to publish, in English,
a study of modern anarchism

D1336105

Richard Gombin

The Origins of
Modern Leftism

translated from the French
by Michael K. Perl

Penguin Books

Penguin Books Ltd,
Harmondsworth, Middlesex, England
Penguin Books Inc.,
7110 Ambassador Road, Baltimore, Maryland 21207, U.S.A.
Penguin Books Australia Ltd,
Ringwood, Victoria, Australia
Penguin Books Canada Ltd,
41 Steelcase Road West, Markham, Ontario, Canada
Penguin Books (N.Z.) Ltd,
182–190 Wairau Road, Auckland 10, New Zealand

Published in Pelican Books 1975
Les Origines du gauchisme copyright © Editions du Seuil, 1971
This translation copyright © Michael K. Perl, 1975

Made and printed in Great Britain by
Richard Clay (The Chaucer Press) Ltd, Bungay, Suffolk
Set in Linotype Times

Contents

List of Abbreviations

BAPU	Bureau d'aide psychologique universitaire (Bureau of University Psychiatric Aid)
CFDT	Confédération française et démocratique du travail (French Democratic Confederation of Labour)
CFTC	Confédération française des travailleurs chrétiens (French Confederation of Christian Workers)
CGT	Confédération générale du travail (General Confederation of Labour)
CMDO	Comité pour le maintien des occupations (Committee for the Preservation of Jobs)
CP	Communist Party
CPSU	Communist Party of the Soviet Union
FA	Fédération anarchiste (Federation of Anarchists)
FCL	Fédération communiste libertaire (Federation of Libertarian Communists)
FO	Force ouvrière (Labour's Strength)
GAAR	Groupes anarchistes d'action révolutionnaire (Anarchist Revolutionary Action Groups)
GIC	Groep van internationale communisten (International Communist Group)
ICO	Informations correspondance ouvrières (Workers' News Service)
IS	Internationale situationniste (Situationist International)

List of Abbreviations

PCF   Parti communiste française (French Communist Party)

PSU   Parti socialiste unifié (United Socialist Party)

RDR   Rassemblement démocratique de la Résistance (Democratic Assembly of the Resistance)

SFIO   Section française de l'Internationale ouvrière (French Section of the Workers' International)

UNEF   Union national des étudiants de France (National Union of French Students)

Preface

Leftism as described and defined in the following pages is first and foremost a theory: a theory of present-day society, of the society of the future and of the transition from one to the other. Very little consideration will be devoted to 'practical leftism', although its haunting presence will be felt behind the text. The reason is that it seemed to me worth while to give an account of leftist theory before embarking upon a description of the practice of confrontation, which at the moment would be fragmentary at best. The theory itself is far from complete, and therefore my principal concern will be with its genesis.

Systematic leftism takes the form of an *alternative* (to use a neologism) to Marxism–Leninism. The interest in analysing it therefore resides in the fact that it presents itself as a successor to a theoretical construction which has practically monopolized radical thought over the last half-century, and which was already the predominant revolutionary doctrine for half a century before that.

The curiosity which modern leftism may excite does not arise simply from the fact that it aims to replace orthodox Marxism as the guiding theory of the revolutionary movement. Other systems of thought have already attempted to supplant it. But most of these *alternatives* have been on the right: social democracy, labourism, cooperation, pro-planning liberalism, etc. Criticisms from the left, that is to say critiques presenting a *revolutionary* alternative, grew out of the same tradition and claimed the same parentage; for the sake of convenience, we shall refer to these as the *extremists*.

Of course there has been anarchism, anarcho-syndicalism, and revolutionary syndicalism. But these movements were the very ones to be ousted from their old entrenched positions by the October Revolution. They were to survive only as minor sects, expending the best part of their energies in pursuing a fanatical critique of the Soviet Union and its supporters. There is no getting away from the fact that for fifty-odd years Marxism–Leninism has reigned supreme, monopolizing the ideological leadership of the organized revolutionary movement.

Opposition was made even more difficult by the intolerance of the communist system's 'guardians of conscience': you were a revolutionary only if you came out in favour of Bolshevism, a counter-revolutionary if you permitted yourself the slightest criticism of Moscow.

Modern leftism has broken this vicious circle, broken cheerfully with Marxism–Leninism, and has assumed the role of inquisitor in its turn. To enhance further the novelty of its new departure, its propagation has coincided with the coming of age of a whole generation of militants who have not had to suffer the traumas of Stalinism, with its absolutist pretensions that elevated it to the status of an eternal truth. Consequently, the theoretical initiative has found a sociological base in a living movement.

Finally, having consigned Marxism–Leninism to the ideological dustbin of history, the modern leftism theory claims to be the expression of current struggle. In this sense, it no longer represents one radical utopia among others, but the *theory* of a revolutionary movement in full flood.

This, then, is the extent of the leftist ambition. It seemed to me essential to present the various aspects of the new current of thought in a succinct form. It must be emphasized that it is new only by virtue of its newsworthiness and by the gradual merging of disparate elements. The reader will recognize some familiar themes, which may remind him of other periods of history. For novelty does not in fact consist in erasing the past and starting from scratch. It is the result of a sudden convergence of a number of currents, previously dispersed or forgotten, with a social reality which appears to justify them. What is new, unprecedented, is the fact that these currents have sprung forth unlooked-for on the scene of confrontation, the fact that they are fed by a common inspiration and, above all, by what I shall call an identical vision of the world, which makes it possible to contain several disparate fragments within the same logical framework.

Leftism, therefore, is a way of thinking, of reacting in the face of the same phenomena, of revolting against all attempts at regimentation. The cohesion of leftism is a theoretico-practical cohesion: theory does not find its justification within itself, but in the action it claims to express.

If the leftists are right, if their theory is really the theory of the real, the actual, it cannot fail to acquire over the years all the attributes of a finished theory. Marxism itself is a synthesis of disparate elements; leftism has not yet found its own synthesis. Will it ever do so? For the moment, we can only trace these elements in outline, while suggesting the Ariadne's thread by which we may pass from one to the other. At the same time, we may sketch the broad features of the recent historical developments that have enabled these elements to emerge.

Introduction

What is modern leftism?

If we consider the whole body of changes which have taken place in every field within the past ten years or so in France, to speak only of that country, we are obliged to recognize that our old habits of thought have ill prepared us to assimilate them.

Whether it be a matter of economic explosion, the massive irruption of children and adoloscents into the schools and universities, the rise of total demand to a hitherto undreamt-of level or the new needs born of the wholesale shift of society to a *quantitatively* higher plane, we are unable to adapt our psychology, our thought and our reflexes to the era of advanced technology (or the 'post-industrial era', as some sociologists like to call it).

If we think that for untold centuries, indeed to the present day in most countries of the world, *life* as defined by a decent standard of consumption (in terms of food, culture and social benefits) was the prerogative of a privileged minority, it may be said that the present epoch is characterized by the irruption of the masses into the domain of *real* life, in other words by their emergence on to a plane where the satisfaction of their minimum needs is conceivable.

In its awareness of this emergence from the realm of scarcity, mankind is impatient to satisfy its needs – all its needs. It is clear that the struggle against the obstacles barring man from enjoying the fruits of his own labour has taken new forms. Seen on the social scale, this means that social struggles have changed both in appearance and objectives.

If we look at the French labour movement from the time of its initial organization in the 1880s (both on a trade-union and a party level) up to the end of the 1950s, it will be seen that it follows a historical line of development starting from a situation of intensive capitalist accumulation and ending up in the age of consumption. Throughout these seventy years, the worker's primary concern was to defend himself against unemployment, poverty, the oppression of the employers, in short against all the hazards inherent in a capitalist economy based on scarcity. The liberal State claimed to maintain a position of neutrality, implying that it was up to the organizations created by the proletariat to fight for the everyday welfare of the worker, and at the same time against a system which *by its very nature* perpetuated injustice and poverty. Accordingly, the trade unions, however staunchly they may have supported a *revolutionary* syndicalism in theory, and despite their ambitious programmes and apocalyptic vocabulary, in fact practised a somewhat milk-and-water reformism. The political parties, which by the end of the century were influenced by Marxism, followed a similar pattern: they offered the masses a revolutionary ideology coupled with a reformist practice (this was as true of the pre-1914 SFIO as it was of the post-1930 CP). The strength of their hold on the masses was in direct proportion to the rigour of their organizational structure. So far as the PCF was concerned, it was still bathed in the glory of a successful revolution, and the extreme subversiveness of its vocabulary was an additional recommendation.

In short, the hold these trade-union and party machines exercised over the mass of the working class was primarily due to the nature of their objectives. Obliged to struggle for *immediate* economic aims in a situation of scarcity, the proletariat cedes its autonomy and delegates its power, all the more so for the fact that the realities of the capitalist market necessitate the organization and concentration of decision-making. To put it in a nutshell, since it was obliged to transform itself into a pressure-group, the working class equipped itself with all the attributes of a pressure-group: leadership, bureaucracy, hierarchy and authoritarianism.

The results achieved (increases in wages, security of employment, social insurance, other legislation beneficial to the proletariat, democratization of the electoral system) corresponded exactly to the needs of a class seeking to win itself a place within the capitalist system. The true extent of these achievements is open to debate, but it is undeniable that the leadership of the working class, charged with managing the immediate interests of that class, carried out its task by managerial methods.

The reason why this hold has lasted for almost a century, and still survives to a degree, is that the problems of economic and job security were an ever-present reality to two thirds of the population – and this is a fact that should not be forgotten.

A course of development that began in 1936 was interrupted by the last war, until the flow of militants to the CP was revived by the Resistance. Subsequently, the liberation of France re-created a situation of economic scarcity, job insecurity and, by way of corollary, a resurgence in the power of the Communist Party and of the unions controlled by it. But as France began to emerge from the economic morass, at the beginning of the fifties or thereabouts, the traditional leadership of the working class, despite their unprecedented power, were quite clearly out of touch with the new aspirations of the workers, directed towards the new opportunities offered by the industrial society. A political structure (the CP) and a trade-union structure (the CGT) based on democratic centralism, that is to say total centralization to the benefit of the party and trade-union machines, a strategy which vacillated between reformism and harassment of the State establishment, these were the norms of working-class organization as seen by the majority of the French labour movement in the years following the liberation.

The gap between the specific needs peculiar to the machines in question and the general needs of the working population rapidly became apparent. Stalinism in its broadest sense was, in the West, a brutal effort to preserve, to freeze for ever a politico-social structure which was after all ephemeral and dated. Organized communism in the capitalist countries had nothing to offer the new needs and aspirations of the workers except intransigence in theory coupled with total compromise in practice. In a world of relative abundance, of unprecedented technological, scientific and economic change, of completely new sociological groupings, the labour movement suddenly and spontaneously rediscovered its most natural, and also most ancient, preoccupations, which the years of 'quantitative' struggle had helped to disguise. The workers, tentatively and uncertainly at first, are beginning to express their will to determine the objectives of this struggle themselves, from the grass roots, and above all to fashion in the society of the future an authentic socialism founded on autonomy of decision, that is to say a decentralized and self-governing socialism.

The new type of social conflict, which for the sake of convenience we shall term '*contestation*'[1] and which has become fairly world-wide over the past few years, emerged in a particularly violent, concentrated and massive form in France with the general strike of May–June 1968.

The *contestation* in these conflicts was aimed at once at the employers, the State authority and the traditional leadership of the workers. By resisting both the repressive structure of society, in whatever part of the world, and the stranglehold of the working-class leadership, the workers were returning to more basic responses that would have been better understood by a Proudhon or a Bakunin than by a Marx or a Lenin. But whereas the Bakuninite critique could only lead to a step backward in the socio-economic context of the time, postulating as it did a collective aspiration towards a more or less mythical past (a society of free and independent craftsmen), the situation today is quite different. For after years of reformism in practice and of dogmatism in visions of the future, many workers now seem ready to assume responsibility for their own destiny and to take the management of their affairs into their own hands. Revolutionary theory is moving in a similar direction: it no longer precedes social action but follows it, or at best runs parallel to it.

The leftist objective, as it may currently be observed, seems to be to provide *contestation* and its protagonists with a theory to embrace their own practice. But 'leftism' is a term both overused and over-abused, so that it is necessary to clarify certain points before proceeding further.

To the political scientist, leftism may be either a portmanteau word (the generally accepted, journalists' meaning) or a tech-

1. For an initial semantic and political approach, cf. G. Lavau, report to the Congress of the AISP, Munich, 1970 (duplicated text).

nical term, with a meaning sufficiently precise to be immediately accommodated in the framework of an analysis which transcends it. Either way, the value of such a concept can only be heuristic, and is in no way essential; hence our definition of leftism is not intended to be exhaustive – quite the contrary; it is restrictive and selective, deliberately isolating a certain number of characteristics.[2]

We shall here refer to leftism as that segment of the revolutionary movement which offers, or hopes to offer, a radical alternative to Marxism–Leninism as a theory of the labour movement and its development. This at once excludes all the attempts at theoretical renewal that have emerged out of social democracy, to the extent that they are not revolutionary (that is to say they do not aim at the immediate and total overthrow of capitalist society). It also excludes all movements of communist *opposition* or a communist renewal, to the extent that they offer no alternative (proposing instead to return to the Leninist or revolutionary sources of communism). To these two 'pure' types one might add a third, situated somewhere between the two; this would consist of the groups which regard themselves as both revolutionary and reformist, which draw both on Bolshevism and social democracy for their inspiration. The French PSU and the British New Left provide a good illustration of this category, and there are other small study-groups which support the revolutionary reformism of A. Gorz, the Italian 'Il Manifesto' movement, or both.

Only the second category seems to require any comment. It is very wide-ranging and includes a number of groups that are commonly lumped in with leftism. It covers all those movements (most of which are quite old) which accuse the CP of having betrayed Marxism–Leninism, either recently (1956) or since 1925 or even 1923. As the reader will have recognized, these groups are the ones consisting of the various internal

2. A. Kriegel has attempted to draw a distinction between leftism and extremism which is very different from this: it does not seem to me to clarify matters to define leftism as a 'safety-valve'; has not communism too been a safety-valve in most countries? *Les Communistes français* (Paris, 1968), pp. 234–5.

'communist oppositions' (represented in France by *Unir-Débats* and *Le Communiste*), the Bordiguists, the Maoists,[3] the Trotskyists, whether Posadist, Frankist, Lambertist or Pablist in tendency. The one feature common to all these groups, beyond their very major theoretical differences, is their reference to Marxism–Leninism and their position in relation to the Communist Party.

By attacking the Party for its betrayal of Marxist–Leninist theory or practice, or both, these groups present themselves as the faithful guardians of orthodoxy. In this sense, they offer an alternative, but an alternative to the leadership of the Party and not to Marxism–Leninism. In this sense, therefore, one may speak of leftism, but it is a leftism in relation to the Party and not in relation to communist doctrine. It thus seems preferable, in the framework of the definition we have given to the leftist concept, to speak of *extremism*, for the objective of these groups is to move to the *extreme* of communist doctrine and not to replace it.

A borderline case is that of the spontaneist Maoists (Mao-Spontex, ex-Gauche prolétarienne, Vive la révolution, etc.) which retained, after May 1968, the tactical spontaneity and the notion of 'propaganda of the deed' derived from the leftists. The presence of Alain Geismar at the head of the ex-Gauche prolétarienne is a good illustration of this marriage of Maoist dogmatism with the spontaneity inherited from the Movement of 22 March. However, to the extent that these groups are only spontaneist at the tactical level, while remaining Marxist–Leninist on the doctrinal level, they will not be included in this study.

Having drawn the distinction between leftism and communist extremism, and having defined it as a practical and ideological alternative to Marxism–Leninism, it only remains to give an

3. Originally, these were against de-Stalinization, against the Russian 'revisionists' and for Mao, the only 'correct' interpreter of doctrine. Since June 1968, the pattern has become complicated by the addition of other elements. The common factor is still that beyond Stalin, Mao or Enver Hoxha, Lenin remains the paragon of the Marxist militant and thinker.

account of its aims and its origins, and to ask where it fits into the tradition of the revolutionary movement.

To the extent that it is a movement *of ideas*, leftism is at once a critique, a praxis and a theory. A critique, firstly, which extends from the revision of Marxism to the point of negating it as a revolutionary theory. In the last analysis, Marx emerges as the theoretician of the bourgeois revolution pushed to the limits of its potentialities. The whole of the Leninist theory of organization, its very conception of revolution as the seizure of political power at the summit, bears all the marks of bourgeois thought. To a leftist, it is therefore not surprising that the Russian Revolution should have resulted in a State-capitalist régime reproducing a more refined and more concentrated version of the system of class domination.

The leftist critique therefore repudiates all the revolutions of the twentieth century, or rather denies them the label 'socialist'; it sees in them the last of the bourgeois revolutions.

This analysis leads to a view of organized communism and social democracy not as deviations from an ideal model, but rather as capitalist institutions, that is to say institutions tending to manipulate capitalist society in the direction of greater efficiency and a greater concentration of power.

Seen in this light, leftism appears as a revolutionary praxis wherever the class struggle breaks the mould previously established by traditional organizations – everywhere, that is, where it is directed both against the system and against the working-class leadership. This praxis is manifested in wildcat strikes, the occupation of factories, takeovers of cadres and organization at shop-floor, factory or company level outside the existing trade-union or political frameworks. A praxis of this type would unmask the oppressive, restrictive nature of the 'historic' instruments of leadership, which faithfully reflect their bourgeois originals. In this perspective, the general strike appears as the first or at least the most extensive demonstration by the workers against their own organizations.

Leftist theory, on the basis of this type of praxis, adopts and puts forward an entirely new historical analysis and projection. According to this view, socialism is no longer to be regarded as a manipulation of an existing model of society, but a higher stage characterized by the autonomy of human groups. The prefiguration of the emancipated society is more or less detailed according to the group and its particular theoretical bent (for leftism is still far from homogeneous), but all leftists are agreed on the principle of autonomy, which consequently excludes all authoritarian, centralist, interventionist, planned and ideological models. 'Ideology' here means the phenomenon of repression in the realm of the mind and of collective attitudes. Just as bourgeois civilization introduced the structure of authority (paternal, managerial, pedagogical, political, etc.), one of its more heinous misdeeds was to sanctify ideological domination. And the revolutionary leaders, with Lenin at their head, conformed slavishly to this pattern by imposing on the proletariat from outside an ideology – the ideology of their own liberation.

The object therefore is not to put forward a new ideology, but to abolish and demystify all ideologies. The ideal activity of revolutionaries will be to systematize, to give some coherence to, the fundamental praxis of *contestation* as it exists here and now. The revolutionaries are therefore concerned to draft a theory for their own practice, without the analysis ever becoming congealed, fixed at a specific historical point, in which case it would become an ideology.

. Here again, all kinds of variations are to be found: from the groups which reject all theorizing and rely on the pure spontaneity of the workers, down to those which postulate the organizational forms which the workers will establish (workers' councils, action committees, etc.). However, there is general agreement on the central revolutionary reality, which is the independent activity of the workers in their day-to-day struggle.

As for the means of establishing the socialist society, they are not to be fixed immutably either: far from conforming to a pre-established organizational pattern, revolutionary activity will create its own forms of struggle in the course of the movement to a *higher historical stage*. In other words, just as socialist society will be characterized by self-government at every level, the revolutionary process will include the totality of individual autonomous struggles. Starting from the hypothesis that a society can only be free if it is freely established, the leftists see in contemporary revolutionary practice a tendency towards autonomy of struggle, towards an instinctive rejection of all leadership and all hierarchies, however revolutionary.

Having projected the principle of autonomy on to its vision of the future, having made this the very essence of the revolutionary process, having aimed at renewing revolutionary thought in its historical dimension by this means, leftism has also found a new conception of the content of this process.

Orthodox analysis on this subject – drawn principally from the writings of the 'older' Marx, from the analysis in *Capital* and in the critique of the Gotha Programme – fixed the revolutionary timetable in advance. The revolution was supposed to come at the climax of the period of capitalist development, when the socio-economic system had matured sufficiently to allow certain factors to come to fruition which the old system already contained within itself in embryonic form.[4] The revolutionary struggle, and the political organization of the masses, appear in this light as both a preparation (notably by education) for the advent of socialism and as a 'hefty shove' to shake the old world on its foundations.

The favoured battle-grounds of revolutionary action are the centres of production. Since all alienation springs from economic alienation, this has to be suppressed first by abolishing wage slavery and collectivizing the means of production. It is therefore no accident that the communist parties have chosen the factory as the base of their organization.

The revolutionary time-scale of leftism emerges as both less determinate and longer than this. An economic evolutionism contradicted by events has been repudiated. On the other hand, a greater place has been reserved for revolutionary voluntarism, and hence for the socialist conscience, although this latter may of course not be imposed from outside. While it is admitted

4. In his critique of the draft Erfurt programme, Engels had already abandoned all the 'revolutionary voluntarism' of the 1840s and 50s, and went so far as to predict a quasi-automatic change-over to socialism, notably in England.

that a capitalist economy is not without internal contradictions, it has become apparent that the system has found a way of taming its crises and learned to prolong its own existence. The end of capitalism is not yet in sight, and can only be foreseen as the result of a constant and conscious struggle, both against the system and against the traditional revolutionary opposition.

But this conception of the revolution, while it may appear more atemporal than Marxism–Leninism, is also much looser spatially, extending far beyond the simple notion of battle for the abolition of the wage bond. For revolutionary action means to the leftists a permanent struggle on *all* fronts. All alienations – psychological, sexual, cultural, ideological and, of course, economic – must be done away with. The front of the revolutionary struggle has thus become greatly extended: the revolutionary process itself has been drawn out both in space and in time. Its ultimate objective is the conquest of all powers, the end of all alienation; something which cannot be achieved within the scope of an insurrection but demands a whole historical period.

It may legitimately be asked whether these few features characterizing the leftist movement are enough to establish it as an entity *sui generis*.

Obviously since leftism categorizes itself in historical terms, only history will provide a definitive answer. The contemporary observer of a phenomenon can only go by the indicators, and the one which seems to us decisive, and legitimizing by the same token this type of study, is that the totality of analyses, reflexes, ideas and practices which I have termed 'modern leftism' do not constitute a phenomenon specific to a given country, nor did they appear suddenly out of thin air. Since the present work is restricted to a study of leftism in France, it will attempt to consider its genesis in this particular instance. Mere superficial observation will show that it represents the point of convergence of a number of currents differing in form, content and aims – currents which, for the most part, often sprang from origins which go back well before the last world war, but all of which became crystallized after 1945. Likewise all, or almost all, of them fused after May–June 1968 in the wider movement of world-wide *contestation*, which thus emerged as the synthesis of these separate individual currents.

If we have not stopped to detail the content of French leftism, this is because the analysis of its various components in the chapters to follow will be concerned with that very question. Before embarking on the study of individual trends, it would be as well to emphasize that the national framework accorded to this book is entirely arbitrary and was chosen for reasons of practical convenience. Not only is leftism not a specifically French phenomenon, but in its role as a revolutionary alternative it has made its appearance in France a quarter of a century late, compared with Central Europe. This is due to various factors, and primarily to the relatively tardy introduction of Marxism into France and to the richness of a specifically national revolutionary tradition. Similarly, at the time when Marxism was beginning to be seriously questioned in the German-speaking countries, it had only just been properly assimilated by French thinkers and was only just finding its first 'high priests' among them. It was indeed in the interwar period that a number of highly regarded intellectuals and philosophers went over to Marxism: whereas before 1914 it had only provided the *inspiration* for a part of the socialist movement, from then on it was to be *a subject for commentary* as well. But no sooner had the Marxian exegesis begun to be introduced (and nourished by the translation, in 1933, of the *Economic and Philosophical Manuscripts*) than the final 'Bolshevization' of the French CP and the Stalinization of its leaders was to petrify Marxist–Leninist theory right up to the 1950s. There was talk of a period of Stalinist 'glaciation' (Edgar Morin), and it is true that only a few intellectual circles outside the Party continued to keep up the interpretative and analytical tradition of the twenties.[5]

5. The question is dealt with by G. Lichtheim, *Marxism in Modern France* (Columbia University Press, 1966). Jean Touchard writes that until 1930 Marx was only known to the French communists through the medium of the October Revolution. It was the 'Philosophies' group that was to discover Marx by way of a philosophical approach and which might have been able to develop a Hegelian interpretation of Marxism, had it not been for the intellectual 'glaciation' of the thirties to which I have referred. See *Le Mouvement des idées politiques dans la France contemporaine* (Paris, Cours IEP, 1968), pp. 22 and 170.

In contrast, a tradition of high-level theoretical Marxian critique has existed in Central Europe since before the First World War. Austro-Marxism and the critique of Lukács gave rise, in the nineteen-twenties and thirties, to a veritable Marxist *revisionism* and even to attempts to transcend Marxism, after thinkers such as Karl Korsch, Pannekoek, Ernst Bloch, Th. Adorno and Horkheimer had drawn up a critique of Leninism as a non-Marxist political praxis, or of Marxism as an analysis unable to give an account of modern industrial society.

It should be added that several abortive revolutions (Hungary and Bavaria, notably) provided examples of a different kind of praxis, of organizational models differing from Leninism (independent workers' councils, for example).

Besides these neo-Marxist explorations, the occupation of factories in Italy in 1919–20 and the Spanish revolution (1936–7) added more fuel to the non-Leninist and even non-Marxist revolutionary tradition.

It is certainly true that in such circumstances the birth of French leftism can only be viewed in the context of these international precedents. But whereas certain analyses involving a break with orthodox Marxism and a search for new departures could be lifted whole from illustrious predecessors like Lukács and Korsch, other aspects of French leftism stemmed more directly from the French tradition, whether literary (Rimbaud, the surrealists) or political (Fourier, Proudhon, revolutionary syndicalism).

In reality, a multitude of trends go to make up the tissue of an intellectual movement that is challenging for the succession to a revolutionary theory identified with the labour movement for more than fifty years. A survey of the various aspects of the phenomenon of leftism, their genesis and their content, will permit a better appreciation of this many-sided phenomenon, which owes it coherence to an apparently fortuitous convergence of various different factors, united nevertheless by a common aim: to change the world and transform the human condition.

1. The vital question

*The régime of the USSR and the phenomenon
of bureaucracy*

In order for the revolutionary movement to be able to attack the Marxist–Leninist 'system', to revise and replace it, a formidable obstacle had to be overcome: the critique of the Soviet revolution. While it is not inconceivable that the CP might have been 'by-passed' to the left in 1938–40, in view of the signs of its more sober approach since the time of the Popular Front and the 'wildcat' methods first introduced in the strike of 1936, the last war and the experience of the French Resistance helped somewhat to refurbish its image. For the generation which came to the Party in 1930, and for that which rejoined it in the Resistance, communism was the incarnation of the doctrines of Marx, Engels and Lenin, as Stalin's Soviet Russia was the logical and legitimate continuation of the Russia of 1917–23. For a wide range of Communist Party supporters, whether manual workers or intellectuals, progressive Party workers or 'fellow-travellers' from the prosperous middle class, the Communist Party was not merely the 'party of the 75,000 martyrs of the Resistance', the party which had contrived to reconcile patriotism with internationalism, revolutionary struggle with governmental responsibility, but also and above all the party connected with the USSR, that country whose enormous sacrifices had made possible the defeat of Nazi barbarism. To the whole world, whether sympathetic or hostile, the Party was the undisputed incarnation of the revolution: its leadership of the working class appeared wholly legitimate, as by divine right.

To contest the Party's 'revolutionary representativity' meant instant ostracization from the movement, and in practice this often meant joining the ranks of the enemy. To thousands of militants, 'to be outside the Party meant giving up the struggle to change the world, it meant a renunciation of all that was best in oneself. It meant sinking back into the petty-bourgeois slime.'[1] Besides, most Party members did not ask themselves too many questions; those who were not members but regarded themselves as revolutionaries or even just 'of the left' were invariably hamstrung by the Sartrean philosophy of commitment: but to be committed between 1944 and the beginning of the fifties could mean nothing other than commitment to the 'Great Cause'. Outside the Party, there was no salvation.

Similarly, the part played by those who attempted to maintain a balance between the rejection of Stalinism and the rejection of pro-American social democracy was extremely difficult to keep up. Yet some mention must be made of the experiment made by Sartre and his friends, for it illustrates at once an attempt at a leftist critique of Stalinism and its dismal failure. The experiment goes back to the tiny movement called 'Socialisme et Liberté' which Sartre had created during the war: it was continued in the creation of *Les Temps modernes* and various attempts at establishing a political footing, among which the Rassemblement démocratique de la Résistance (RDR) had some ephemeral success.

Whereas the RDR was doomed from the start, because of the very fact of its heterogeneous composition, *Les Temps modernes* survived, but the experiment it represented (the attempt to keep at an equal distance from communism and the 'bourgeoisified' socialism of the SFIO) was a failure: of its four founders, three (R. Aron, A. Camus and M. Merleau-Ponty) veered towards liberalism, while the fourth (Sartre) became, according to some, the 'Enlightened Companion' of the CP,[2] or according to others an uncompromising Stalinist who had been of greater service to the Party from the outside than he ever was from within.[3]

However that may be, *Les Temps modernes*, by its readiness to inform its readers on the reality of the Stalin régime (camps,

---

1. E. Morin, *Autocritique* (Paris, 1959), p. 159. The best analysis of this state of mind among intellectuals is that by D. Caute, *Communism and the French Intellectuals* (André Deutsch, 1964).

2. S. de Beauvoir, *La Force des choses* (Paris, 1963).

3. J. Ardagh, *The New French Revolution* (Secker & Warburg, 1968), Chapter 11.

trials, dictatorship) and by its penetrating analyses, was able for a time to play the role of left-wing critic and tarnish the idyllic image of the Soviet Union entertained in left-wing circles in France. The theoretical debate introduced by the review from 1945 was aimed at a readjustment of Marxist theory to the current facts: it started out with a rejection of the Communist Party's yesmanship, its blind allegiance to the policies of Stalin.[4]

During the first period, which lasted until 1952, various voices could be heard, often discordant, sometimes going so far as to question Bolshevism itself. Those who moved the furthest along this road, and who were to make a reappearance in *Socialisme ou Barbarie*, were attempting to consider Stalinism in a new light: not as an accident attributable to Stalin's personality, but as an inevitable development of a bureaucracy inherent to the Bolshevik Party. Since the 'committee-men' first took over the controls of the Russian Social-Democratic Party in 1901, the Party cut itself off from the will of the masses, and the leaders even found themselves in opposition to the masses during the decisive periods of struggle in 1905–7 and in April 1917.[5] This kind of analysis gives a relativist view of the Bolshevik revolution, in fact the reflection of a backward capitalism, almost an accident of a history temporarily twisted out of shape by the will of Lenin.

The whole process which led to Stalinism was therefore fully in keeping with the image of a party completely removed from the masses, a party which had been forced to make itself authoritarian, centralist and bureaucratic in order to 'short-circuit' the gradual processes of the masses. By the same token, no Bolshevik could exempt himself from the accusation of bureaucracy, least of all Trotsky. The so-called degeneration of the Russian Revolution had been the product of the Party itself, and Stalin was cast in the image of that Party.[6]

4. M. Merleau-Ponty: 'Pour la vérité', *Les Temps modernes*, 4 (1946).

5. Benno Sarel: 'Lénine, Trotsky, Staline et le problème du parti révolutionnaire', *Les Temps modernes*, 73 (November 1951).

6. Cl. Lefort: 'La Contradiction de Trotsky et le problème révolutionnaire', *Les Temps modernes*, 39 (January 1949).

This critique of Bolshevism led on to an analysis of the Soviet Union to which few of the collaborators of *Les Temps modernes* were able to subscribe, since it called in question the socialist nature of Russian society and presented Stalinism as a system of exploitation even more highly developed and refined than the classic form of capitalist system.[7]

It is true that a tendency less critical of the journal's editorial team began to question the concept of liberty as understood by the Soviet leaders. After the revelations about Soviet internment camps, Sartre went so far as to admit 'that these facts (massive deportations) place the whole meaning of the Russian system in doubt'.[8]

Nevertheless, this 'centrist' trend,[9] of which Jean-Paul Sartre, from the height of his enormous prestige as a libertarian writer and philosopher, was the very incarnation, hesitated to draw all the conclusions which these revelations, among others, might be thought to entail. This Sartrean group, obliged to recognize the reality of oppression in the Soviet Union, the gap between the ideal and everyday practice, nevertheless opted for the latter, since it aligned itself with the progressive forces of this world and to take a stand against the USSR would mean alliance with her enemies.

Whereas Sartre, finding it impossible to maintain a position in unstable equilibrium between criticism and praise, deviated gradually from this perilous standpoint towards total alignment with the CP and 'fellow-travellership',[10] Merleau-Ponty, after following a different path, gradually moved towards the standpoint of bourgeois liberalism. The importance of his

7. cf. in particular, besides the articles of Benno Sarel and Cl. Lefort already quoted, the latter's 'Sociologie du communisme', *Les Temps modernes*, 50 (December 1949).

8. J.-P. Sartre and M. Merleau-Ponty: 'Les Jours de notre vie', *Les Temps modernes*, 51 (January 1951).

9. From which Raymond Aron cut himself off from the start, attracted as he was by British Labourism, which he considered to have effected the takeover from the ruling class 'without any rupture or upheaval'. 'Chance du socialisme', *Les Temps modernes*, 2 (1 November 1945).

10. cf. his article 'Les Communistes et la paix', *Les Temps modernes*, 84 (November 1952).

approach to a critique of the Stalinist system arises from the manner in which he formulates the problem: he sees it as a whole, instead of attacking one or other particular aspect. He recognizes the seriousness of the facts and the violence. He is also ready to excuse this violence (of which no-one was innocent, as he accepts, least of all Trotsky), on condition only that it leads towards a new humanity.[11] By asking this crucial question, he shook the very foundations of Bolshevism, even despite himself, before the 1950s. He was thus a part of the movement of leftist criticism of Bolshevism and the Soviet Union, and gave it a new philosophical dimension that was rare at that time.

But Merleau-Ponty's critique, drawn up in the form of a series of questions, became bogged down in an apparently unending chain of further questions, to the point at which their author broke with the revolution. By contrast, the Trotskyist critique, although part of a much more specious viewpoint, was at the same time far more fruitful, since it made it possible to attack Bolshevism without abandoning its revolutionary premises.

Trotskyism, therefore, provided leftism with its point of attack: Soviet bureaucracy. In a sense, Trotskyism itself started out as a form of leftism: by questioning the very structure of the Soviet régime, the Trotskyists started from a foundation which might have led to a critique of Leninism itself. However, they were never able to take this vital step, for they based their whole attitude on a single magic – and arbitrary – date, 1923, before which everything was roses, while after it everything began to go wrong.[12] By virtue of this one fact, Trotskyism has more the characteristics of extremism than of leftism, to apply the distinction drawn in the Introduction.

11. cf. his article 'Pour la vérité' quoted above, and his book *Humanisme et terreur* (Paris, 1948), where the subject is dealt with in greater depth.
12. This was not the only obstacle: the Trotskyists reproduced in their very organization a Leninist, even a Stalinist, model, so precluding any development in this respect.

So while the attempted critique by *Les Temps moderne* seems ambiguous, holding a very precarious balance between Stalinist orthodoxy and liberal thought, Trotskyism was the only movement in the immediate postwar period to sustain a serious left-wing critique of Stalinism.[13] Organized Trotskyism and notably the PCI (International Communist Party), was also to provide the sounding-board for the political opposition to Stalinism: the reasoned negation of Leninism was constructed on the basis of Trotsky's ideas, but was also to be directed against them.

The condemnation of Stalinism as a caricature of socialism meant making a serious bid to challenge the Soviet régime. This is what Leon Trotsky dedicated himself to from 1923 onwards, from the formation of the Left Opposition in the Soviet Union. Between 1923 and 1940 he developed an analysis of great penetration which led him, on the basis of an exhaustive description of Soviet society, to state that the Soviet State under Stalin remained a workers' State; that Russian society was still very close to the Marxist model, but that its socio-economic régime was a transitional one between capitalism and socialism. Its transitional nature was, according to Trotsky, the result of the inadequate development of the factors of production on the one hand, and the existence of a bureaucratic stratum at the summit of the social structure on the other.[14] The ruling caste had taken over the apparatus of the State, had secured for itself all the privileges, carved itself the lion's share in the distribution of the national income and almost restored the conditions of a thoroughgoing exploitation. Nevertheless, having completed a description of Soviet society which has since become a classic, and from which it emerges that inequality, poverty, prostitution, abuses of every kind had made their reappearance in the Soviet Union, from which, above all, it emerges that the group in power possessed all the features of a dominant group, Trotsky concludes that the Soviet bureaucracy is *not* a class in the true sense. Although it had raised itself up above other groups in society, although it was a

13. E. Morin, *Autocritique*, p. 77.
14. L. Trotsky, *The Revolution Betrayed* (Pathfinder Press, 1972); see in particular Section IX: 'What is the USSR?'

privileged and dominant' group, differing from every other
bureaucracy in that it served only itself, it had not created any
social base for its domination. In particular, since it did not
own the means of production, and could not bequeath its goods
and its privileges, it remained a *political* and not a social
phenomenon.

To reach this conclusion, Trotsky had started from a highly
literal interpretation of Marxism, according to which it is the
ownership of the means of production which characterizes
régimes. Since Marxism knows no other form of ownership
than individual or collective, Trotsky defined the USSR as a
degenerate workers' State, the base of which was socialist, but
with a mode of distribution which was bourgeois and operated
to the benefit of a tiny minority. This situation, according to
him, could only be unstable and transitory; the régime would
sooner or later have to move in the direction of complete
socialism or tip backwards to capitalism. In the former case,
it would probably need a *political* revolution; in the latter case
a complete *social* counter-revolution would be necessary, since
the relationships of production would have to be altered.

Whatever the value of this analysis,[15] it became, after
Trotsky's death in 1940, the bible of all those who attached
themselves to his cause.

After the war, this analysis came to appear both to go beyond the theses of the CP, in that it called Stalinism in question and aspired to a return to the pure and healthy springs of
Leninist Bolshevism, but also as less far-reaching than some
views which detected in Stalinism something other, and more,
than a mere political structure.

Nevertheless, by his attack on Stalinism, supported by his
personal prestige as the companion of Lenin, Trotsky had
opened a breach in the monolithic structure of world communism, and through this breach poured every radical critique
of Stalinism.

Within the Fourth International, after 1944, and in its

15. It has some glaring weaknesses: how could Trotsky, good Marxist
that he was, so readily accept that an economy with a socialist base
could produce a superstructure (i.e. the bureaucracy) so utterly non-
socialist?

French section, the PCI, it was assumed without question that the Soviet State was both proletarian and degenerate, half-way on the road between capitalism and socialism. But Trotsky, as we have seen, considered this state of affairs to be abnormal: the régime of the USSR seemed to him to be in unstable equilibrium; it was fated inevitably either to develop towards socialism or to 'fall back' into capitalism. The war, he was convinced, would precipitate this development: the USSR could only emerge from it as a fully fledged proletarian State, or slide back into the barbaric state of capitalism.

However, come the Liberation, not only was this 'unstable' régime in better health than ever, but the leaders of the Fourth International 'froze' any new interpretation of this phenomenon by attributing to Trotsky's analyses the qualities of an unassailable dogma. This situation drove a number of young Trotskyists to form a splinter group, which claimed that the analysis of the Russian régime and its bureaucracy should be carried further in the light of the new facts. Going back to the reasoning of the founder of the Fourth International, they came to the conclusion that the Stalinist bureaucracy had become a true *ruling class*.

The revolt and the subsequent breakaway by the young Trotskyist dissenters in 1948 was apparently based on a point of secondary importance: the designation of the Soviet ruling group. In fact, the real issue was the whole Trotskyist doctrine, which the expellees, grouped around the review *Socialisme ou Barbarie*, were subsequently to condemn as 'ideological conservatism'.[16]

Taking issue with Trotskyist dogma, which saw in Stalinism a phenomenon that was purely political and nothing else, *Socialisme ou Barbarie* asserted that the Russian bureaucracy was a veritable ruling *class*, oppressive and exploitative, the social expression of new economic forms and new models of exploitation.[17]

16. Cl. Lefort: 'Organisation et Parti', *Socialisme ou Barbarie*, 26 (November–December 1958).

17. cf., for example, *Socialisme ou Barbarie*, 1 (March–April 1949), Editorial; and 9 (April–May 1952).

This was now a real innovation in the framework of Marxist theory, since a third socio-economic category had been created, besides free-enterprise capitalism and socialism.[18] This new category was State capitalism, resulting in a form of development common to all the industrialized countries and all modern societies, and which had its origins in the world of before the Great War. This development is characterized by an increasing concentration of property in the hands of those who also control the management of commercial enterprises and hold the reins of State. The bureaucracy is the *new class* which benefits from this development: it achieves the ambition of every capitalist, for it is the sole and undisputed wielder of economic and political power; it has no trade-union opposition to cope with, let alone political opposition.

By comparison with the bourgeoisie of the Western countries, the Stalinist bureaucracy possesses one peculiarity which might at first sight seem to deny its class nature: its members are not individually owners of the means of production. To the *Socialisme ou Barbarie* group, this is not a decisive argument, however. For a start, the Russian bureaucracy possesses all the attributes of a property-owning class – it decides upon and directs investment, fixes prices and wages, appoints and dismisses local functionaries and enjoys a standard of living and a way of life which in the West would be the apanage of the bourgeoisie. At all events, and this is the second point, it controls the means of production and enjoys the attendant privileges *collectively*: but this is merely a question of legal status which in no way alters the bureaucracy's real situation as a class. Besides, in the capitalist countries it is no longer true today that the property-owning middle classes are the major beneficiaries of class exploitation; it is the executives and managers of industry and commerce and the higher civil

18. In the early days, the review and the group hoped to remain within the limits of Marxist thought; indeed, the traces of Trotskyism were never entirely to disappear. Thus in the nineteen-fifties P. Chaulieu reiterated the analysis of the Russian bureaucracy as the result of a degeneration of the October Revolution, 'Réponse au camarade Pannekoek', *Socialisme ou Barbarie*, 14 (April–May 1954).

servants who corner the benefits of the system, and this not b[y] virtue of a formal title to property, but from the fact of thei[r] situation in the productive set-up.

The bureaucracy of the Eastern countries thus possesses al[l] the characteristics of a dominant class: from its existence, th[e] analysts of *Socialisme ou Barbarie* deduce that the Sovie[t] Union is a *society of exploitation* and that the Soviet State i[s] a *capitalist State*.[19]

Certainly this analysis of bureaucracy is not entirely novel[;] quantities of ink have flowed on the subject, from Hegel['s] *Principles of the Philosophy of Right* down to Djilas's *Th[e] New Class*. But Lenin and Bukharin, Max Weber and Trotsk[y] all considered the problem from the political angle. Onl[y] Roberto Michels had gone one step further, by asserting tha[t] the management of an enormous volume of capital gave th[e] managers a power comparable with that enjoyed by the actua[l] owner.[20] But the first man to speak of 'bureaucratic collec[-] tivism' and explicitly to designate the Russian ruling group as [a] *class* was Bruno Rizzi, who expressed these ideas within th[e] framework of a critique of Trotskyism when he left the move[-] ment just before the war.

In his dispute with Trotsky, Bruno Rizzi maintained[21] tha[t] the Soviet State is not a workers' State because the capitalis[t] class has not been replaced by the working class but by th[e] *bureaucratic class*, which includes State and Party officials[,] technicians and experts of every kind. He estimated this new[,] ruling class as comprising fifteen million people, and the share[,] of production monopolized by them on the eve of war at 4[0] per cent.[22] This class corresponds to a new form of socia[l] organization and results from a considerable growth in th[e]

19. Besides the articles already quoted, see P. Chaulieu, 'Sur le conten[u] du socialisme', *Socialisme ou Barbarie*, 17 (July–September 1955).

20. For a historical analysis of the various concepts of bureaucracy, se[e] P. Naville, 'La Bureaucratie et la révolution', *Arguments*, 17 (firs[t] quarter, 1960).

21. Bruno Rizzi, *La Bureaucratisation du monde* (published privately[,] 1939).

22. ibid., pp. 21–4 and 83. This estimate is the same as Trotsky's, wh[o] backed it with detailed statistics: op. cit., pp. 138–41.

orces of production, which excludes, according to Rizzi, any likelihood of a return to capitalism in the USSR.

The divergences with Trotsky are therefore apparent; but it was on the basis of the latter's analyses that Bruno Rizzi (who had already evinced an intuitive perception of the new Russian ruling class in 1936, in his *Où va l'URSS?*) was to give a closely reasoned development of his thesis, and indeed he himself readily acknowledged the debt.

While it may thus be affirmed that the analysis of the Russian bureaucracy as a *class* springs from a common source (Trotskyism), from which both Rizzi and the founders of *Socialisme ou Barbarie* had drawn in abundance, and while we may even assume that the former had some influence on the latter, the differences of detail and, above all, the clearly contradictory conclusions drawn by the two parties from these common premises should not be overlooked.[23]

Whereas Rizzi lumped together the Nazi and fascist régimes with that of the USSR, applying to all three the term 'bureaucratic collectivism', the collaborators of *Socialisme ou Barbarie* regarded the fascist bureaucracy as a purely political phenomenon, since private property and its individual beneficiaries still existed; this was not the case in the Soviet Union, where the very form of property had been modified. The chief point of difference, however, is that Rizzi, convinced of the convergence of all types of régime towards bureaucratic collectivism, remained highly sceptical of socialism's chances of ever winning the day. Consequently he even went so far as to propose an alliance between the proletariat and fascism to oppose capitalism.[24] The collaborators of *Socialisme ou Barbarie*,

23. *La Bureaucratisation du monde* was published by the author in 500 copies. The war and Trotsky's death prevented discussion of the ideas contained therein during the 1940s. Chaulieu may possibly have known of it (a fact which seems to be suggested by the author of the article 'Les classes sociales et M. Touraine', *Socialisme ou Barbarie*, 27 [April–May 1959], note 13).

24. Rizzi, op. cit., Chapter 7. One might also mention Rizzi's violent anti-semitism ('The struggle of National Socialism [against the Jews] ... is practically just' – p. 295), which was not shared by *Socialisme ou Barbarie*.

on the other hand, considered socialism inevitable, and looke
on their task as a preliminary demystification necessary to ar
reconstruction of revolutionary theory.[25]

For this reason, their analysis did not confine itself to a
examination of economic and social relationships in th

25. The all-embracing nature of the analysis undertaken by *Socialism
ou Barbarie* and the political conclusions which that group drew from
mark it off straight away from this review of theories otherwise close to
It should not be forgotten that the discussion of the nature of th
Russian ruling group had not ceased to preoccupy Trotskyist circles th
world over since the beginning of the nineteen-thirties. Their origins ma
be traced to the platform of the Workers' Opposition in 1921 (repre
duced in *Socialisme ou Barbarie*, 35 [January–March 1964]). The Trotsk
ist Rakovsky wrote in 1929 that the bureaucratically deformed State o
the USSR had turned into a bureaucratic State. Trotsky took up th
analysis on his own account (in *The Revolution Betrayed*) but drew n
conclusions from it. Thus B. Rizzi was simply continuing in the sam
tradition, only he carried the discussion on to a higher plane (Trotsk
was to acknowledge as much in *The USSR in War*, published in Se
tember 1939). By contrast, James Burnham, Max Schachtman and othe
merely copied Rizzi's arguments; cf. P. Naville's article in *Argumen*
quoted above and I. Deutscher, *The Prophet Outcast* (Oxford Universit
Press, 1970), p. 463.

In fact James Burnham's theory of the 'managerial revolution' fal
well short of Rizzi's analysis in the poverty of the concepts it employ
and in the series of hypotheses it postulated which subsequently prove
false. Incidentally Burnham abandoned not only Marxism but the revolu
tionary movement: he came to deny any possibility of socialist revolu
tion, on the grounds that the proletariat does not have ownership o
the means of production in bourgeois society, and consequently has n
opportunity of reinforcing its position as a class, in contrast to th
bourgeoisie under the feudal system. J. Burnham, *The Managerial Revo
lution* (Penguin, 1962), pp. 69–70.

The difference between *Socialisme ou Barbarie* and a man like Burn
ham is that the latter regards bureaucracy as a necessary parasitic phen
omenon arising out of the technical requirements of a modern economy
The analysis given by *Socialisme ou Barbarie*, by contrast, concludes tha
it is a social phenomenon comprehensible only in the context of th
development of the class struggle in modern society. As Lefort ha
written, *Socialisme ou Barbarie* begins its analysis where Burnham lef
off; see 'Sur l'article de Morin', *Arguments*, 4 (June–September 1957).

As for Milovan Djilas's book *The New Class*, it provides an illustra
tion of these considerations, but at a very crude conceptual level. It
chief value is as a personal testament, but even from this angle it i
disappointing.

USSR: since it was supposed to provide the fundamentals of revolutionary theory readjusted to fit contemporary reality, it went further than this. It endeavoured to answer the question 'Why was the class hatched by the October Revolution a new class? Why was there no Thermidor, as Trotsky had maintained, i.e. a simple about-face?' In order to answer this fundamental question, it was necessary to take a closer look at the bureaucratic phenomenon, to ask oneself if it represented an accidental, specifically Russian social form, or whether it represented a new, universal category which made it possible to understand the development of modern capitalism. Detailed study of the Russian economy, the social and economic relationships characterizing Soviet society, shows that it is going through the last phase of capitalist development – that in which the development of technology has reached a peak, in which the concentration of capital and of power is at its most intense. P. Chaulieu has deduced from this that the bureaucracy is that precise class that corresponds to this stage in the development of capitalism, and that it has its roots in the absolute concentration of economic and political power in the hands of the Party. Now the concentration of political and economic power is a phenomenon which also characterizes the capitalist countries of the West – the only difference is that in these countries it is not yet absolute. In this sense, the countries of the East present a picture of a concentration that is complete – perfect, one might say, from the point of view of a French, English or American industrialist. There is nothing to stand in the way of the march of the economy and the reality of exploitation: neither opposition parties, nor trade unions, nor even quarreling capitalists. Just as it wants an entirely controlled economy (a process already begun by monopolistic mergers, nationalization and State controls), the bourgeoisie aspires to become a bureaucracy. In this sense, it may be said that the bureaucratization which is a reality in the Eastern countries is an irresistible tendency in the countries of the West.[26]

26. See, in particular, Chaulieu, 'Sur le contenu du socialisme', *Socialisme ou Barbarie*, 17 (July–September 1955), and A. Garros, 'L'Union de la gauche socialiste', 26 (November–December 1958).

At this point, it may well be asked whether modern burea
cratic societies or societies in the process of bureaucratizatic
have preserved all the classical features of exploitation: i
dividual appropriation of surplus value by the owner of tl
means of production. By virtue of the fact that the bureaucra
operates as a collective entity, and because of the separation,
the West, of the functions of management and of ownershi
the decisive boundary is no longer that between the propert
owner and the propertyless but that between management ar
operatives.[27]

Whereas the contradictions postulated by classical Marxis
(between the individual nature of property and the soci
nature of labour) have been muted in the new situation whio
applies in all the developed countries, new contradictions ha
been introduced which the system cannot and never will r
solve: the contradictions which result from the total cleava
between managers and workers, and which present-day capita
ism must preserve in order to survive. The worker reduced
the condition of a mere robot, with no power of decision
control over his own actions, also loses his spirit of creativi
and will tend to abandon all initiative in his work. But sino
the system of production is becoming technically and intellect
ally more and more complex, it can only continue to functio
with the active and willing assistance of those very peop
whose personalities are being eradicated. Consequently, th
system needs a spirit of initiative in its workers in order
function; but if it were to acquire such a spirit, the ruling cla
would lose its permanent basis of domination – the separatio
of management and work-force.

27. J. Burnham was well aware that property and management n
longer coincide, but his analysis is impaired both by a number of fal:
predictions (such as, for example, that of general unemployment in th
capitalist countries) and by the purely circumstantial conclusions h
draws from them, notably those relating to the existence of manager
the social basis for which he completely fails to demonstrate. *Socialism
ou Barbarie*'s analyses of modern capitalist society may be found in th
collected articles of P. Chaulieu: 'Le Mouvement révolutionnaire sou
le capitalisme moderne', Nos. 31, 32 and 33 (December 1960, April
June 1961 and December–February 1961–2).

What interests us here is not to verify the accuracy of this
analysis or to compare it with the facts, but to see in what way
it has made inroads on orthodox Marxist analysis and, above
all, to see how it has inspired and given consistency to a new
revolutionary theory. The renewal (or revision, depending on
the standpoint of the observer) of Marxist theory with regard
both to capitalist society and to the society calling itself socialist
is too obvious to need further emphasis; the lumping together
of the régimes of East and West, their integration in a system
of bureaucratization founded on new social relationships is of
the very greatest interest for the development of leftist ideas.
True or false, *Socialisme ou Barbarie*'s analysis of bureaucracy
is the only one that exists, if we exclude liberal thought on the
one hand and Marxist–Leninist thought on the other. But the
most striking and interesting feature of the approach consists
in the *potential* development it allows. Such developments relate
to three essential aspects of the leftist movement:

(1) the application of the bureaucratic pattern to modern
society and the contemporary labour movement;

(2) the content of socialism as it appears in the (perhaps
negative) light of the experience of Bolshevism triumphant;

(3) the conclusions which may be drawn from it with
regard to the forms of organization of the revolutionary
movement.

These are all questions which lie at the very heart of leftist
theory; we shall return to them after considering the philosophical critique of Marxism.

2. Philosophical revisionism

Modern leftism, in that it is an attempt to renew the theor
and practice of revolution, can only be a success if it engage
in a ruthless critique of the Marxist–Leninist system, tha
system which has monopolized revolutionary thinking sinc
1917. More than this, leftism is first and foremost the absolu
negation of any revolutionary ideology (ideology being unde
stood in the sense of 'false consciousness'). The first obstacle i
encountered at the level of the Soviet social system; this pre
sented itself to the world as the epitome of socialism. Th
picture was marred somewhat by the analysis of the bureau
cratic class. It was further spoilt by contrasting Marxist though
with the model pretending to incarnate it. This confrontatio
with the facts led to a *philosophical revisionism* of Marxisr
itself, an attempt to return to the original springs of Marxism
In the past, any work which aimed at re-launching revolution
ary thought came up against the totalitarian pretensions (in th
etymological sense) of 'orthodox' Marxism, which presented it
self as a closed, scientific and final system. Not only all socia
life but all the sciences were contained by this veritable *cos
mogony*, with its own holy writ, its official priesthood, its devia
tions and its heresies. The important thing was to break th
vicious circle, to crack the monopoly of theory held by th
high priests of communism. Revision, then, consists of Marxis
self-questioning; an application of Marxist methods to the ver
content of the doctrine. In France this work is associated wit
the name of the journal *Arguments*, founded at the beginnin
of 1957. In fact, of course, the *Arguments* team had no mon
opoly of doubt on the subject of theoretical Marxism, anc
moreover the solid content of its revisionism is very poor. O
the other hand, this journal put the problem very clearly anc
its chief merit lay in having enabled the French public to be
come familiar with the experiments in revisionism carried out ir

entral Europe in the twenties and thirties. So it was not so
uch a matter of revising as of evoking a revision already
rried out thirty years earlier, of presenting and translating
xts hitherto unpublished in France.

This time-lag is an interesting phenomenon. Why did it take
ch an unconscionable time to tackle the basic philosophical
oblem, which consisted in surpassing Marx's economic analy-
s, the strategic and tactical thinking of Lenin, the totalitarian
ctatorship of Stalin in order to arrive at the philosophical
vel reached by Marx and Engels in the period from 1843 to
48? The delay was primarily due to Marxism's late introduc-
on into France, and to the simplified and schematic form
which this took place.[1] It is also due to the existence of
authentically French socialist tradition which was very
ep-rooted in the urban proletariat. The great majority of
ilitants only knew of Marxism through the October Revolu-
on. Subsequently, in the course of the nineteen-twenties, a
hole constellation of left-wing intellectuals discovered Marx
a Hegel and deepened the philosophical dimensions of his
aching.[2]

However, their membership of the Communist Party marks
e cessation of all philosophical thought throughout the thir-
es, forties and fifties, the years of 'glaciation' as E. Morin
lls them.[3]

The chief reason for the time-lag was thus the Party's ab-
olute authority in matters of ideology. Not until the liberation
f France was there any attempt at *philosophical revisionism*.

1. See the latest work on the subject: M. Dommanget, *L'Introduction
u marxisme en France* (Paris, 1969).
2. The best-known of these included Lefebvre, Politzer, Guterman and
riedmann, all members of the 'Philosophies' group. All went over to
e Communist Party and abandoned their philosophical research. Cf.
an Touchard, *Le Mouvement des idées politiques dans la France con-
mporaine* (Paris: Cours IEP, 1968), which sheds valuable new light
the subject, notably on pp. 22 and 170. Cf. also the memoirs of H.
efebvre in *La Somme et le reste* (Paris, 1959).
3. We should not overlook Alexandre Kojève's lectures (1933–9) en-
led *Introduction à la lecture de Hegel*, or the works of Lucien Gold-
ann. However, their impact at the time was minimal.

Merleau-Ponty was by that time asking questions of Marxis which were truly philosophical, examining the finality of Stali ist violence and, on the eve of the Twentieth Congress of th CPSU, writing that in order to understand the famous Stali ist 'degeneration' it was necessary to go back, not to the origi of Bolshevism, but to the well-springs of Marxism itself.[4] Th he was himself to do, basing his attitude on the writings of G Lukács and K. Korsch and ending up by denying dialectic materialism. But Merleau-Ponty's analysis was that of a disap pointed man, who was ultimately to seek a 'reconciliation' wit bourgeois liberalism. *Les Aventures de la dialectique* contai the seed of all future debates, but it was not until the Twentiet Congress, Poznan, the workers' councils of Hungary and th intervention of Soviet tanks that a mass of communist inte lectuals were to give in to a kind of collective catharsis whic enabled them to denounce the gods they had previousl adored.

What led them to re-examine hitherto unquestioned stand points was the 'exploding' of Stalinism, as it was called by th editorial to the first issue of *Arguments*.[5] The editorial team first intention had been to seek, under the innumerable layer of the Marxist–Leninist palimpsest, the first, original scrip This meant going back to first principles, denouncing scholasti cism, 'de-dogmatizing' knowledge, questioning Marx's though by applying his own method to it.[6] But the effects of the gran revisionist design entertained by *Arguments* did not entirel measure up to expectations; notably the philosophical discus sions never reached a level comparable with that of the pre-wa German school; the revisionism of *Arguments* was entirely on of form and not of content, for which one had to consul Lukács, Adorno and Marcuse. The old vigour was missing Marxism was too compromised, associated as it was with totali

---

4. *Les Aventures de la dialectique* (Paris, 1955), p. 116.

5. *Arguments*, December 1956–January 1957. The editorial board of th French edition included C. Audry, R. Barthes, J. Duvignaud, E. Morin These were later joined by K. Axelos and P. Fougeyrollas.

6. J. Duvignaud: 'Marxisme: idéologie ou philosophie', *Arguments*, (February–March 1957); E. Morin, 'Révisons le révisionnisme', ibid.

tarian forms of government, and it seemed as though no philosophical renewal could imbue it with new life.[7]

In order to understand the meaning of the philosophical revision of Marxism, and remembering that the stakes were the emergence of a new theory of the proletarian movement, it should not be forgotten that orthodox Marxism had set itself up as a 'scientific' system well before the advent of Stalinism. It was therefore not enough to demonstrate the extreme poverty of Stalinist philosophy, it was still necessary to go back to its roots. This meant the necessity of applying to Marxism its own analytical concepts, in fact to undertake the same operation as Marx did when he examined the meaning of the German philosophy of his day. Now Marx's *critical* method is that of his philosophical writings, where he used the dialectic as a category of logic. It was therefore vitally necessary to re-examine the philosophical writings of the young Marx, his Hegelian origins and, of course, his development.

But in the years which followed the Russian Revolution, this kind of undertaking was by no means an obvious necessity, since the 'official' Marxism that had come to be accepted was that of *Capital* and Engels's *Anti-Dühring*. The heritage which had been assimilated was that of the critique of political economy, the enunciation of laws governing trends (fall in the rate of profitability, concentration of capital, proletarization of the masses, inevitability of economic crisis). Marxism had been turned into an economic determinism of universal validity; a science of society and social development; a set of laws which need only be consulted in order to determine whether or not a revolution has any chance of success, or whether a party is opportunist, adventurist or simply counter-revolutionary. This system, as has been said, was something of a cosmogony, since

7. In fact, there were a number of phases: up until 1960, the aim was revision properly speaking (the expression was first used by E. Morin in *Autocritique* (Paris, 1959), p. 241, in which he speaks of 'total revisionism'), after which Marxism was quite simply abandoned and a new search for a 'planetary' system of thought integrating the acquired knowledge of the social sciences into its conceptual apparatus was set in motion; cf. 'L'Evolution d'*Arguments*' by Y. Bourdet in *Communisme et marxisme* (Paris, 1963).

it even applied to the natural sciences: the dialectic, which has become the supreme science, governed the development of things (dialectical materialism) as well as of beings. Consequently it was possible to have anti-Marxist sciences, or, on the other side of the fence, Marxist interpretations of genetic (Lysenko).

The 'scientistic' and economic interpretation of Marxism goes back, without doubt, to the last period of the writings of Marx and Engels. It is not necessary to consider here the validity of 'Marxian' theories according to which Marx is supposed to have been betrayed by his epigones, starting with Engels, and again according to which the economist Marx had never renounced the philosophical work of his youth, etc. What is of chief interest here, by contrast, is to establish the origin of the 'scientistic' trend.

There is certainly no doubt that Engels had been attracted by the natural sciences all his life, and had shown marked positivist tendencies. It was he, therefore, who gave the most complete account of dialectical materialism, and although Marx declared himself to be in entire agreement with it, it was in fact Engels's text which provided the work of reference for the German Marxists of the end of the nineteenth century. Engels regarded the dialectic as the science of the general laws of movement and development of nature, of human society and of thought. Its central principle he saw as negation, and he gives concrete examples, even extending into mathematics (the multiplication of two negative values gives a positive value: $[-x] \times [-x] = +x^2$).[9]

8. The best presentation of Marxism as a system hinging on a number of different phases is still that by George Lichtheim, *Marxism* (Routledge, 1964), which distinguishes a 'pre-Marxist' Marx who develops, after 1860, towards economism.

9. F. Engels, *Anti-Dühring* (Paris, 1950; Lawrence & Wishart, 1955); cf. esp. Chapter 13. The book first appeared in German in 1878, and was more widely read than *Capital*. It was through *Anti-Dühring* that a whole generation of German socialists first became acquainted with Marxism. Actually, Engels states that Marx had never applied the dialectic to anything but history, but he adds that 'it [the dialectic] would seem to be a self-evident feature of the natural sciences'.

Besides this, Engels predicted the consequences of the economic development of advanced capitalist régimes (the United States, France, Great Britain) and came to the conclusion that socialism would come about of itself, by the natural and necessary process of evolution.[10]

By virtue of this approach, he broke very explicitly with the voluntarist period of Marxism, that of the *Communist Manifesto*, but also broke off relations with Blanqui, and put forward a determinist and evolutionist theory which applied as much to things as to thinking beings. On the philosophical level, this expressed itself in the form of a rather sketchy materialism, in which matter becomes a category apart, an absolute of which consciousness is only the reflection. The dialectic, having become the science of nature, was removed from the dimension of philosophy and gave way to the concept of the 'reflection'.

After Marx's death, Engels set about propagating the whole of this bundle of concepts, transmitting them notably to his spiritual heir, Karl Kautsky. Lenin in turn took Kautsky as his model, 'guided' in this by the philosophical conceptions of Gyorgy Plekhanov. In his great philosophical work of 1908, *Materialism and Empiriocriticism*, he was to prove much more of a materialist than a dialectician, and his ideas reflected, as we shall see, the scientistic positivism of the nineteenth century.[11]

The symmetry between the Kautskyist and the Leninist interpretations of Marxism stops, however, at the philosophical level. Both were convinced that dialectical and historical materialism represented the *realization* of philosophy which Marx had prophesied. But on the political scale, or if one prefers on the level of revolutionary praxis, Kautsky (and

10. F. Engels, 'Critique of the Draft Erfurt Programme' (1891), in Marx–Engels, *Critique of the Socialist Programmes of Gotha and Erfurt* (Paris: Spartacus, 1948), p. 73.

11. It is true that Lenin, in his *Notes on Hegel's Dialectic*, returns, after Plekhanov, to a more Hegelian view of the dialectic; but it may be noted that all he, or Plekhanov, retained of Hegel was the attempt to found a dialectical philosophy of nature, not its application to the world of the mind.

German social democracy with him) remained the circumspect evolutionist, waiting for the time when German society would of its own emerge into the Democratic Republic,[12] while Lenin by contrast, proved to be an ultra-voluntarist, the natural successor to traditional Blanquism. In other words, Lenin broke all ties between doctrine and political action, whereas his 'orthodoxy' in matters of philosophy enabled him systematically to underestimate the independent role of the proletariat, since the strict determinism to which he attached himself gave the right to interpret the laws of the historical dialectic to the 'guardians of bourgeois science'.[13]

The mechanistic materialism of Lenin, who saw the origin of all phenomena in matter (understood in the physical sense) had the further consequence of entirely separating being and consciousness, of making one the reflection of the other, and hence of denying all class consciousness that was independent of and did not flow from those who *knew* how to interpret the laws of scientific socialism – the professional revolutionaries.[14]

It will be seen that such a conception, which freezes the dialectical processes (and which, it should be noted, represents a return to the Kantian thing-in-itself) resolves itself, in the last analysis, into a simple causal determinism, the precise image of the positivist conceptions of the last half of the nineteenth century. It makes it possible to enunciate eternal laws (dogmas) specifying at the same time that they may only be accepted or rejected *en bloc* (the latter alternative being necessarily counter-revolutionary). Here, then, is the seed of ideological totalitarianism, and it only remained for Lenin's successors to

12. As Engels had taught; cf. the 'Critique of the Draft Erfurt Programme' already quoted.

13. His ideas on political organization and action, which derive from the position analysed above, may be found in *What is to be Done?* (1902).

14. It is significant that from 1919, the Bolsheviks insisted on presenting the programme of the Russian Communist Party as having a 'scientific character', drawn from Marx's correct observation of the capitalist régimes (which he is supposed to have examined as one might examine a clock, the defective functioning of which enables one to predict that it will shortly stop): N. Bukharin, G. Preobrazhensky, *The ABC of Communism* (Penguin, 1969), pp. 66–7.

pursue the propositions contained in this 'orthodox Marxism' to their logical conclusion.

When, in 1923, Georg Lukács published a volume of studies on Marxian dialectics, it was not his intention to contradict the extollers of 'scientific' Marxism, but to apply the dialectic to social phenomena, and first and foremost to *class consciousness*.[15] Nor was Karl Korsch, in his *Marxism and Philosophy* published the same year, any more concerned to criticize the Authorized Version directly: he simply put the question of the link between the philosophy of the proletariat and the social revolution.[16]

In the last analysis, these two books have the same object: to apply Marxist (dialectical) method to the development of Marxism; consequently, and to simplify this account, we shall give a schematic analysis of this, for the features which are of concern in the present work are the conclusions that were subsequently to be drawn by the leftists with regard to the problem of revolutionary theory.

Both attack the materialist notions of contemporary Marxists, which separate matter from spirit, making one a simple reflection of the other. This philosophical assertion, which provides the basis for the primacy of the substructure over the superstructure, is not dialectic, for the conscious activity of an individual is on the objective side of the *process*, a datum which Lukács contrasts with both being and consciousness.[17] Only the process is an objective reality, for in it subject and object, being and consciousness are united. 'We find the subject

15. *History and Class Consciousness* (Merlin Press, 1971). Lukács contrived at the same time to maintain that Lenin was a great philosopher, which is difficult to reconcile with his trenchant critique of dialectical materialism.

16. K. Korsch, *Marxism and Philosophy* (New Left Books, 1970). In the first edition (1923) he was extremely prudent, and refrained from attacking any interpretation; in the second (1930), on the other hand, he launched a frontal attack on Lenin's materialism. For the purposes of the present account, there is no need to give a chronological chart showing the development of his thinking. Consequently we shall henceforth refer to the second edition, that of 1930.

17. On the whole of this passage, cf. G. Lukács, op. cit., p. 165.

and object of the social process coexisting in a state of dialectical interaction.'[18] So much so that even the simple fact of the knowledge produces an *objective* change in its object. To stop at the reality of the mere object would be to grasp only the appearance of things, and this would mean staking everything on their immediacy.

The only valid philosophical category is *totality*, and only by dialectical method can totality be appreciated, whereas the method which Lukács calls 'reflective' only apprehends a false objectivity. The latter is the logical method of the bourgeoisie, which cannot transcend immediacy because it is the prisoner of its position, whereas the proletariat, by the specific dialectic of its class situation, is moved to find a way out of it, since it alone possesses the understanding of the process, hence of the totality. In this conception, consciousness is not a simple reflection of the process of history, but is truly the agent by which history may be transformed: at the moment of revolution the separation between subject and object disappears completely; a fraction of humanity perceives the totality and thus raises itself to the level of self-consciousness.

This represents a positive return to the younger Marx, still impregnated with the philosophy of Hegel, who rejected the Kantian distinction between 'is' and 'ought'. The question for him, and for Marx, is resolved in the notion of historical 'presence' (Dasein).[19]

The identity of subject and object in the process is categorically opposed to the materialism of a Kautsky, a Plekhanov or a Lenin. It is true that Lukács does not make a frontal attack on Lenin, aiming rather at the German reformists, whose theory of evolution without revolution is a direct consequence of the separation of the dialectic from historical materialism. But by accusing Engels of 'ambiguity' in his notion of the thing-in-itself, of having considered concepts the reflections of 'real' objects, he called in question the whole basis of 'scientific socialism'. He does not hesitate to write that the dialectic of

18. loc. cit.

19. On the Hegelian influence on Lukács, see G. Lichtheim's small volume *Lukács* (Fontana, 1970), Chapter 4.

nature leads on to a *pre-Hegelian* materialism which becomes
a form of 'inverted Platonism'.[20] On this point, Korsch is more
explicit in accusing Lenin of returning purely and simply to
Kant. By separating being and consciousness, not only does
Lenin deny any dialectical relationship between theory and
practice, but he also makes being, the 'is', into an absolute –
and ideal – category.[21]

It is evident that the philosophical argument boiled down to
an assessment of the revolutionary movement, and of whether
it is or is not an independent agent of the historical dialectic;
it is the very primacy of the Party which is here in question,
since it is the proletariat as a class which is able to grasp and
overcome historical realities, starting with its own alienation.[22]
In other words, the essential element in historical evolution
does not consist in the contradictions between the forces of
production and the relationships of production, but in the proletariat's consciousness of this. The proletariat's awareness of
the contradictions is not direct; it appreciates them only through
its own alienation. The decisive factor in social change is therefore *alienation* (or, as Lukács calls it, 'reification'). It is no
longer a question of objective, observable factors which may
be deduced from the laws of the dialectic, as the ortho-
doxies (whether Leninist or Kautskyist) maintain, but of a
factor of consciousness, a superstructure. This is very important, and not just in order to understand the vigour of communist attacks on Lukács, but to the very comprehension of
leftism itself, which, as will be seen, places very great importance

20. G. Lukács, *History and Class Consciousness*, p. 202. In this passage,
Lukács bases himself on the *Theses on Feuerbach*. Cf. the interesting re-
flections of L. Goldmann on Marx's monism in these theses, which throw
light on the Lukácsian interpretation ('Philosophy and Sociology in the
Works of the Young Marx', a text reproduced in the anthology entitled
Marxisme et sciences sociales (Paris, 1970), pp. 130–50).

21. K. Korsch, *Marxism and Philosophy*, p. 117.

22. It should be pointed out that Zinoviev was right when he stated in
1924 (at the Fifth Congress of the Comintern) that the theoretical revisionism of the 'two professors' (Lukács and Korsch) represented a threat
to the *existence of the international communist movement*. Quoted by
M. Watnik: 'Relativism and Class Consciousness: Georg Lukács', in
L. Labedz (ed.), *Revisionism* (Allen & Unwin, 1962), p. 146.

on alienation in its vision of capitalist society and its overthrow, both as a universal, omnipresent phenomenon and as
one which is directly communicated to the consciousness of
the workers, without benefit of any privileged intermediary.[23]

In rediscovering the philosophical dimension of Marxism,
revisionism also questions the very meaning of revolutionary
theory. Korsch is far more explicit than Lukács, but his reasoning follows on from their common conception of philosophy
as the spiritual expression of the world. Theory, says Korsch,
is nothing other than the general expression of the real movement of history.[24] Ideology, on the other hand, is thought congealed into a fixed pattern, which no longer expresses a living
reality. This definition, drawn directly from Hegel's definition
of philosophy ('an epoch captured in a thought') and which
Marx was to apply to the movement of thought in his own
time, enables Korsch to apply himself to a dialectical examination of Marxism. Is it still a theory of the development of
the proletariat, or is it, by contrast, an ideology in the Marxian
sense (false consciousness) in that it disguises true social relationships and the true course of historical development?

The importance of this distinction must be emphasized at
once; it makes it possible to unmask a supposedly immutable
system, and hand down to leftism the Korschian concept of
revolutionary theory, defined as the current praxis of the proletariat. At the time when he was writing his *Marxism and
Philosophy* in 1923, Korsch limited himself to applying this
concept to the history of Marxism, in which he distinguished
three phases. The period from 1843 to 1848 was that in which
Marxism expressed the revolutionary tendencies of the European proletariat; 1848 up to the end of the century corresponded to the rise of reaction and the weakening of the class
struggle. Marxism then became critical of political economy

23. In particular, we shall find how much the situationist theory of
alienation owes to Lukács. There is little point in making explicit the
concepts of alienation and reification as used by Lukács. The interpretation the modern leftists were to place on them is what concerns us
here.

24. K. Korsch, *Marxism and Philosophy*, p. 102.

and enunciated the theses relating to *peaceful evolutionism.* From the end of the nineteenth century an attempt was made to return to revolutionary Marxism (Lenin, Rosa Luxemburg).

Whereas in the first period the Marxist critique was a totality (philosophical, economic, political and ideological), in the second period it gave special weight to the economic element, becoming a scientific critique of the economy of a bourgeois State but not necessarily leading to a revolutionary praxis. To convince oneself of this, says Korsch, one need only compare the *Communist Manifesto* with the programmes of the European socialist parties, both East and West.[25]

Subsequently, Korsch, having broken with the KPD (German CP), pushed his analysis even further, showing that Marxism was tainted with Jacobinism from the start, because it stemmed from the philosophy of the bourgeois revolution.[26] Because it remained faithful to the political forms of the bourgeois revolution, because it overestimated the ability of the State to act as the decisive instrument of social revolution and because it identified the development of the capitalist economy with the social revolution of the working class, Marxism became a brake on the revolution; from being a revolutionary theory, it became a pure ideology.[27]

While the transformation of Marxism into a scientific system based on economic evolution still expressed a degree of reality in the course of the second phase, the 'congealing' of this line of thought from the end of the nineteenth century onwards was to establish a final divorce between Marxism and reality. According to Korsch, Bernstein's reformism better expressed the reality of the German labour movement before the First World War than did Kautsky's intransigent and 'orthodox' scientism. Similarly, in the interwar period, Marxism became estranged from social struggle: it had built itself up into a State philosophy, while 'proletarian communism', as a theory of

25. K. Korsch, *Marxism and Philosophy*, p. 57.
26. See 'Thèses sur Hegel et la révolution', Appendix to the French edition of *Marxism and Philosophy*: *Marxisme et philosophie* (Paris, 1964). The German text dates from 1932.
27. 'Dix thèses sur le marxisme d'aujourd'hui' (1950), ibid.

the real labour movement, only seemed to survive thanks to isolated thinkers or groups like the council communists.[28]

The full importance of Lukács's and Korsch's revisionism is evident: most significant is the return to philosophical analysis which resulted from it, i.e. to reflection on Marxism using its own concepts (the dialectic). The outcome of this was a *relativization* of revolutionary ideologies which produced the exact opposite of Marxism–Leninism: whereas the latter presented itself as *the* revolutionary theory, incontrovertible because *scientific*, Korsch saw all revolutionary thought in a dialectical relationship with the real class movement, so defining it as necessarily changeable as that movement changed.[29]

While Korsch and Lukács were making a philosophical critique of Lenin's materialism, it is interesting to compare it with the epistemological theories of the times (the second half of the nineteenth century and the beginning of the twentieth). This analysis is all the more valuable for the fact that it was carried out by Anton Pannekoek, whose political notions of working-class praxis are central to the current theoretical renewal, and whose scientific credentials have never been questioned.[30]

Pannekoek, an astronomer with a world reputation, shows in a very concise study of Dietzgen, Mach and Avenarius carried out in the light of modern epistemological notions (the theory of relativity) that the matter which provides the key concept of Lenin's work is a mere abstraction. Consequently Lenin, who criticizes Mach and Avenarius for their subjectivism (according to which reality is composed of purely mental sensations or elements), has failed to reach the level of their systems. Avenarius considers the dualism between the central nervous

28. K. Korsch, 'The Philosophy of Lenin', article in *Living Marxism* (1938), reproduced as an appendix in A. Pannekoek, *Lénine philosophe* (Paris, 1970).

29. It should be noted that Lukács's conception was much more dialectical, since he does not recognize any social reality separate from its theory, the one transforming the other continually so that together they form the historical *process*, the only objective reality.

30. A. Pannekoek, op. cit. The text was first published in German in 1938, under the pseudonym of J. Harper.

system and the sensations, which, according to him, are only variations of it; Lenin regresses in time, by comparison with this notion, by identifying *nature* with *physical matter* and by creating an absolute opposition between matter and ideal, energy and consciousness.[31] But the whole development of modern physics, says Pannekoek, rejects the material notion of matter (which refers to ether, atoms and molecules), imposing an *abstract* concept instead, one of energy, waves and light. In short, the thing-in-itself is nothing without the representation of it we ourselves make: matter is everything which actually exists, whether in nature or in our own minds.

Lenin, following Plekhanov, regresses towards a *realist* concept of matter as a thing which may be touched, apprehended with the senses. That is to say he returns to the simplistic notion of matter entertained by the bourgeois materialists such as Feuerbach and Büchner, ridiculed by Marx in his philosophical writings.

Pannekoek, it is true, does not content himself with demonstrating the distance between *Materialism and Empiriocriticism* and the concepts of modern physics; he explains why Lenin does not counter Mach and Avenarius with the results of the theory of relativity (developed in 1905 before the publication of Lenin's book), but with the simplistic and outdated materialism of the bourgeois ideologues. The latter was founded on the natural sciences, on which capitalism had constructed the whole of its system of production (and hence of exploitation); what the proletariat needs, on the other hand, is historical materialism, the science of society which reveals to it the true relationships within the capitalist system and hence its own class position.

The revolutionary intellectuals, Lenin among them, struggled in Russia against tsarist absolutism, whose religion provided

31. ibid., pp. 71 and 78–81. As early as 1924, Korsch had shown, without as yet questioning Lenin himself, that when the 'official' thinkers of the Comintern reasoned as materialists, the result was pure positivism. When they thought as dialecticians, their dialectics were nothing more than Hegelian idealism; cf. 'Lenin und die Komintern' in *Die Internationale* of 2 June 1924.

a secular support; it was a first priority to attack this religion, oppose it with earthly, material and scientific truths. The proletariat had first to complete the work of an inadequate middle class, it had to struggle against feudalism and its prejudices – it was necessary to find a philosophy suited to the needs of practical activity. The struggle of the Bolsheviks was similar to that previously carried out by the bourgeoisie of Western Europe, and it is therefore not surprising that the conceptions propagated by Lenin should be similar to those of a man like Feuerbach.[32]

This attack on the orthodox version of Marxism, this confrontation with the Bolshevik ideology both on the level of a dialectic critique and on that of the development of the natural sciences also form, if not the framework, at least the outline of what has come to be called French revisionism. But we should hasten to add that the latter came into being at a very peculiar time, at a time when many illusions which might still have been legitimate in 1920–30 had been destroyed. French revisionism was the direct consequence of de-Stalinization, but at the same time it is the work of one-time Stalinists. Hence its demands (total revision), hence also its limitations. Revisionism adds nothing to Marxism, but by reviving the Central European revisionism of the twenties and given the context of the fifties and sixties, it was to make its own contribution to the grand enterprise of philosophical liberation.

Marxism–Leninism regarded itself as a cosmogony, a total scientific system, that is to say, it presented itself as the embodiment of the philosophy which Marx proclaimed in his 11th thesis on Feuerbach, as the final reconciliation between theory and practice. By showing that far from embodying it, the communists had perpetuated it in a mock-scientific form (in the USSR, in China, in the people's democracies)[33] and

32. A. Pannekoek, *Lénine philosophe*, pp. 99–102. K. Korsch also thinks that Lenin never philosophized in order to 'discover the truth' on any given question, but to settle a dispute with the enemies of the Party. 'Good philosophy' was whatever was useful to the Party. *Marxism and Philosophy*, pp. 109 ff.

33. K. Axelos: 'Y a-t-il une philosophie marxiste?' in *Arguments*, 4 (June–September 1957).

transformed it into an ideology (or, in the Marxian sense, a false consciousness), revisionism 'unblocked' revolutionary thought, at least in so far as it presented itself as a totality. Hence, revolutionary thought was enabled to start functioning again. For revisionism was a radical phenomenon: it wished to return to the root of things, to go over the Marxist critique once more in all its stages.[34] It may be said that it overshot its mark: its original aim, to rediscover a 'pure and primitive Marxism', was never achieved. *Arguments* 'surpassed' Marxism in a non-revolutionary sense; modern leftism, for its part, used it as one of many stars in its theoretical firmament.

The end of theoretical Marxism in France was almost con-temporaneous with its propagation: the paradox is only ap-parent, if one considers that revisionism coincided with de-Stalinization, the workers' councils in Poland and Hungary with 'peaceful coexistence', a thoroughgoing nonsense from the point of view of revolutionary theory.[35]

This destruction of Marxism opened the way to new projects on the level of pure theory. We have seen that *Socialisme ou Barbarie* had been engaged in such projects since 1949. But the group had remained the prisoner of its Trotskyist origins and the atmosphere of its time (the Cold War). The end of the fifties, in contrast, opened new horizons: the multiplicity of new journals and groups, the appearance of new ideas bear witness to the fact.

The movement from a critique of Marxism to the develop-ment of a critique of society and a theory of revolution was to take place gradually, almost unnoticed, starting with the revisionist project and the analysis of Russian bureaucracy. The most obvious novel feature of this new thinking was the break with the old obsession with economic factors. Here again, revisionism contributed to demonstrating that the suppression

34. 'From the critique of heaven down to the critique of earth', as noted in K. Papaïoannou, *L'Idéologie froide* (Paris, 1967), p. 187.

35. J. Duvignaud, 'France: Neo-Marxists', in Labedz (ed.), *Revisionism*, p. 315. In Germany and Hungary, on the other hand, revisionism co-incided with a period of revolutionary effervescence (the Hungarian revo-lution, the Spartakists, strikes in the Ruhr, the occupation of factories in Turin, etc.).

of economic alienation does not bring about the disappearance of all alienation.[36] In other words, the whole heritage of economic determinism was to be rejected, even to the extent that the development of facts and of the sciences had failed to confirm the hypotheses of *Das Kapital*.

In place of the *economism* popularly attributed to the last period of Marx's life, and which ignores the conscious part played by classes and by men while at the same time providing nourishment for an 'ideology of commandment',[37] leftism was to put the freedom of choice of the alienated man to seek his liberation within everyday life.

36. P. Fougeyrollas, *Le Marxisme en question* (Paris, 1959), p. 27. On the transition between revisionism and more recent forms of theoretical criticism, cf. G. Lichtheim, *Marxism in Modern France* (Columbia University Press, 1966), pp. 183 ff.

37. cf. 'L'Expérience prolétarienne', an unsigned editorial in fact written by C. Lefort in *Socialisme ou Barbarie*, 21 (November–December 1952).

3. A critique of everyday life

The period from 1957 to 1962 set up a beacon in the history of French leftism. Stalinism and the political régime of the Soviet Union and the people's democracies had finally been discredited during the preceding decade; nobody on the extreme left of the political spectrum considered it any longer advisable to cite Soviet 'socialism' as an example, and the analysis of socialist bureaucracy was no longer needed.

The revelations of the Twentieth Congress of the CPSU and the events in Poland and Hungary in 1956 gave renewed substance to a critique which was in danger of running out of steam. Direct knowledge of the 'abuses' of Stalinism both in Poland and Hungary,[1] the denunciation of the régime by the very Poles, Hungarians and Yugoslavs who were at once its official representatives and its victims, led to doubts and questions as to whether the superstructure alone was conceivably capable of secreting so many misdeeds, so many crimes. It has been shown that out of this crisis revisionism was born, and that it set about attacking the sacrosanct doctrine itself. The 'destructuring' project was complete: those who had initiated it often exceeded the aims which they had originally set themselves. It now fell to others to take up where they had left off. For these, the immediate task was to fill the immense void left by the relentless critique of Marxism–Leninism and the régime which claimed to embody it.

In the first place, the revolutionary phenomenon needed to be placed in its historical context. Orthodoxy claimed that

1. 1956–8 was a period of new discoveries. The West discovered the East, and the East discovered the West. As happens in every phase of revolutionary agitation, a greater measure of freedom of speech began to be exercised, which enabled the French left to familiarize itself with life and ideas behind the Iron Curtain. Every journal had its own reportage, and some of these make highly instructive reading.

economic contradictions lay at the root of all social change: this logic demanded the overthrow of economic and social structures.[2] Leftism disputes this strict economic determinism. It observes that Western society hardly seems to be on the verge of *the* great economic crisis, the apocalyptic catastrophe which Trotsky was still prophesying in his *Transitional Programme* of 1938.

Having drawn definitive conclusions from the 'socialist' experience of the USSR and the people's democracies, the leftists went so far as to maintain that the mere modification of sub-structural factors (such as collectivization of the means of production, for example) was not enough either to liberate man or to emancipate society.[3] On one point, the critique of bureaucracy had been convincing: the subjection of man is the same – in differing degrees, but no different in kind – in Moscow, in New York or in New Delhi. To the extent that the forms of production and consumption have developed, and to the extent that technology is playing an ever-increasing part in the very organization of society (and hence in the organization of exploitation and oppression), new forms of alienation have appeared.

Every revolutionary project therefore required that a profound analysis of modern society and the forms of alienation secreted by it be undertaken. The light of theoretical analysis was thus redirected from the study of economic factors (mode of production, law of diminishing returns, etc.) towards the *critique of everyday life*.

The critique of everyday life, being the central core of the new radical theory, presented itself as an *absolute* reaction

2. Or their gradual transformation. It is remarkable that modern socialists (from Scandinavian-style labourism to attempts at renewal like those of the New Left or PSU) which claim that they have broken every link with Marxist–Leninist orthodoxy actually emphasize the fetishism of the structure. In the last resort, their socialism boils down to a programmatic demand for 'structural changes'.

3. On this point, see the final dissipation of last illusions in No. 8 of *Socialisme ou Barbarie* (January–February 1951) – R. Bourt, 'Voyage en Yougoslavie', and H. Bell, 'Le Stalinisme en Allemagne orientale'; cf. also in No. 19 (1956), C. Lefort, 'Le Totalitarisme sans Staline'.

against Stalinist dogmatism and its lackeys in France. As H. Lefebvre has pointed out, the postwar generation of left-wing intellectuals was impotent to solve the theoretical problems which presented themselves: either they took refuge in the dogma of the Party, or they sought their inspiration in the unreal, in abstractions; the concrete, the everyday things, things that existed and could be changed, escaped them.[4] At the same time, this critique marked a complete break with all that had gone before: it aimed at being the critical theory of the modern world, and the surpassing of that world. At the basis of this lies a reflection on the modern world, a reflection which H. Levebvre christened 'La Modernité' in 1946.[5] The modern world is one of accumulated production, in which abundance, if not yet actually realized, is clearly visible on the horizon. The enormous increase in cumulative production, the unprecedented progress in technology and science which characterize modern society (in its more advanced sector) give a hint of what is possible. There is, however, a distinct gap between the sector of technology and production and that of private life. The latter is far from following the same path as the former: on the contrary, it is stagnating. Here the gap is all the greater, and all the more keenly felt, for the fact that the possible is not attainable. Here man's alienation reaches its peak.

No critical reflection accompanies this separation between man and the products of his labours; on the contrary, the more deeply man becomes buried in his alienation the more conformist he becomes: contradiction has been replaced by the cult of the new for its own sake (modernism), typical of a world which has lost its poetry.

Certainly the Romantics had already called in question a world that was both technological and boring; but they were only able to resolve the contradictions of their time *ideally*, by grafting on to real life as they actually lived it an imaginary

4. H. Lefebvre, *Critique de la vie quotidienne* (Paris, second edition, 1958), pp. 250–51.
5. cf. the first edition of the *Critique de la vie quotidienne* (Paris, 1947).

life, lived in their thoughts.[6] But their work, continued by Lautréamont and Rimbaud, among others, rapidly degenerated into verbalism and turgidity by the end of the nineteenth century. Dadaism and surrealism administered the *coup de grâce* to the language of alienation by destroying it. Then surrealism itself became lost in the world of artistic creation. Lefebvre concluded by 1946 that it was up to *avant-garde* groups of young people to continue the work begun by their celebrated ancestors.

Surrealism, which began to founder before the war in an academism which became almost respectable after the Liberation,[7] in turn created rebels against its own conformism. Immediately after the Second World War, a phenomenon comparable with dadaism arose: an attempt at the total sabotage of art, at finding a style of life which enriches the real world, etc. Clearly, these new 'fumblings and stammerings' were no more than a pale copy of the project of Tzara and Hulsenbeck, but they had the advantage that they relaunched a handful of young people on the search for the absolute. The most striking personality of these years was Isidore Isou, a Romanian by origin like Tristan Tzara. He defined the creative urge as the essential need of mankind: man raises himself through creation, so making himself a kind of god. Isou propagated his ideas through the medium of the *Mouvement lettriste*, which he founded in 1946. Their immoderately abstruse content did not hold the attention of the young dissenters for long. Nevertheless, the various *avant-garde* movements which finally led to the dissenting generation of the sixties were originally based on the lettrist movement.[8] To some, lettrism represented an assault on culture; these founded the *Internationale lettriste* in 1952 (and broke with Isou), endeavouring to destroy art by the re-

6. This is particularly evident in the case of Baudelaire; cf. H. Lefebvre, ibid.

7. To convince oneself of this, one need only read the book, partisan though it is, of J. L. Bédouin, *Vingt ans de surréalisme (1939–1959)* (Paris, 1961).

8. On the *Mouvement lettriste* and the *Internationale lettriste*, see some fragmentary pieces of information in J. L. Brau, *Cours, camarade, le vieux monde est derrière toi* (Paris, 1968), pp. 59 ff.

direction and projection of a liberating ideal of city planning. The *Internationale lettriste* politicized and researched a *way of life*. A merger of the *Internationale lettriste* with two other *avant-garde* groups gave birth to the Situationist International (the IS) in 1957. In the years that followed, the IS was to attempt an analysis of the modern world from the point of view of everyday life.

The influence of H. Lefebvre is undeniable (and reciprocal), but that of the dadaists, the surrealists, the lettrists and other *avant-garde* groups was also apparent. This current, cultural in origin, was to take up the Marxist critique once more, in particular that portion of Marx that was Hegelian in origin, as interpreted by Lukács.

For the Situationist International, life in modern society could be reduced to *survival* (life brought down to the level of economic imperatives). Such societies are societies of the quantitative, the consumable. Consumption and survival are assured by the Welfare State: that is the only existence permitted, and only such permission is attainable in it.[9] What is the consumer society? It is the society run on the basis of an *economy of consumption* which is the successor to the economy of production. It is characterized by a frenetic production of goods. But this accumulation of production, despite the riches poured out on the world, does not allow the economy to change the world except in an economic sense. Enrichment only results in an expansion of survival, leaving the quality of life untouched. For the quantification of exchange operations, taken to the extreme, reduces man to the level of an object, and renders everyday life utterly banal: both space and time have been telescoped by capitalist production into an 'immobile monotony'.[10] This applies across the board, including tourism, which imitates the circulation of goods with its 'package

---

9. For the main features of the situationist analysis, see G. Debord, *La Société du spectacle* (Paris, 1967); R. Vaneigem, *Traité de savoir-vivre à l'usage des jeunes générations* (Paris, 1967); and the twelve issues of the journal *Internationale situationniste* (recently republished in full by Van Gennep, Amsterdam, 1970).

10. G. Debord, op. cit., p. 137.

tours', its excursions lacking any element of surprise, its factitious recreations. Town planning is the concentrated embodiment of the identification of life with a mere side-show, a monotonous existence devoid of imagination.

The decline and decomposition of everyday life are part and parcel of the transformation of modern capitalism. In the producer societies of the nineteenth century (whose rationale was capital accumulation), merchandise became a fetish, in that it was supposed to represent a product (an object) and not a social relationship. In modern societies, where consumption is the *ultima ratio*, all human relationships have been modelled on this pattern: all have been impregnated with the rationale of mercantile exchange. Life is thus experienced at one remove, it has become a show in which everything is becoming incorporated. This is the phenomenon to which the situationists refer as a *spectacle* (Lefebvre's concept is more neutral: the modern spectacle, to him, simply arises out of the contemplative attitude of its participants). The show is established once merchandise comes to occupy the whole of social life. Thus in a merchant–showman economy, alienated production is supplemented by alienated consumption. The modern pariah, Marx's proletarian, is no longer so much the producer separated from his product as a *consumer*. The exchange value of goods has finally ended up by dictating their use. The consumer has become a consumer of dreams.

In addition to this, it must be said that the show society, originally the product of a developed economy, has spread to the underdeveloped countries which, although they lack the material base for a social organization of this type have nevertheless imitated the showman techniques of their sometime colonizers. Everywhere, from now on, whether East or West, the quantitative rules, a guiding principle of life; the economic imperatives impose their scale of values on the whole of life. 'Only the object is measurable, which is why exchange reifies.'[11]

Despite this devastating critique of the consumer society, the situationists are careful to avoid contempt for consumer goods

11. Vaneigem, op. cit., p. 89.

as such. They consider that it is not their consumption which is alienating but their *conditioned choice* and the ideology leading to it. For everyday life in the modern world is subject to a 'totalitarian management' which shapes the very models of our behaviour.

It is evident that in this analysis of alienation, the situationists and H. Lefebvre are developing the thought of the younger Marx, notably the *Economic and Philosophical Manuscripts*. They derive their arguments on the reification and fetishization of material goods from the passage in *Capital* entitled 'The Fetish of Material Goods and its Secret'.[12] But they do not claim to have made the only correct exegesis of Marx: in fact they go beyond Marx, and are not Marxists in the modern sense. Their notions of Marxian theory broadly follow the pattern first laid down by K. Korsch, discussed earlier. Their 'surpassing' of Marx consists in the fact that whereas to Marx separation was still circumscribed to the world of production, to them it has become universalized; the whole of social praxis has been split down the middle, into reality and mirage. Between man and his work, man and his desires and dreams, a number of mediations have been interposed. In a society run by cybernetics (the society towards which we are moving) the power of organization will have replaced the power of exploitation: the alienating mediations in such conditions are multiplied to the point of paroxysm. In the extreme case, the masters will themselves become slaves, mere levers of the organization.

The critique of everyday life is not intended to be purely an analysis; it is supposed to lead on to a revolutionary praxis. The transition from one to the other is facilitated by the existence of contradictions in the modern world. The great contradiction which undermines the consumer society results from the fact that cumulative production has unleashed forces which destroy

12. *Capital*, Book I, Part 1, Chapter 1, iv. It is interesting to note that to the 'orthodox' Marxists this very passage is out of tune with the rest of *Capital* and the works of Marx's maturity: 'Last trace of the Hegelian influence, extremely damaging' (L. Althusser, Explanatory Note on *Capital* [Paris: Flammarion, 1969], p. 22).

the economic necessities. The internal rationale of the system requires an infinite economic development, and only the quantitative and consumable are actually supplied to the individual. Once primary needs have been fulfilled to saturation, new pseudo-needs are 'manufactured' (a second car, a better refrigerator, down to the ultimate gadget which is no use for anything). This process causes an accelerating degradation of everyday life. But at the same time, tremendous technical strides give a glimpse of new worlds, of unsuspected means of gratifying unknown desires. Consequently the critique of everyday life is initially carried out from the *inside* – it is the critique of the 'real by the possible'.[13] The extent and point of attack of this internal criticism vary according to viewpoint: H. Lefebvre indicates a degree of optimism when he affirms that it is by and through leisure that modern man will express his revolt against the break-up of his everyday life and the way it is being made increasingly banal. The situationists think that recreations themselves have become alienated, and that they, too, should be opposed.[14] However, there is agreement on the hard core of the contradiction inherent in anything that is *everyday*: the forms of life must enter into conflict with its content; there is a separation of form and content.

This contradiction produces a consciousness of separation, a sufficient ground for discontent and a revolutionary praxis. But a difficulty arises here: opposition to the dominant class is not easy, for that class is itself mystified. The spectacle has invaded not only society but also its contradiction: opposition has become just as much a matter of spectacle (ideological in the Marxian sense). In other words, side by side with the pure acceptance of the 'silent majority' there is a purely contemplative revolt. Dissatisfaction itself having become frozen into a piece of merchandise, the dissatisfied man finds it difficult to emerge from his role of dissatisfied man. Technical civilization,

13. H. Lefebvre, *Critique de la vie quotidienne* (second edition), Foreword, p. 16.
14. However, Lefebvre's ideas go further than the view of sociologists like G. Friedmann who contrast leisure and work, stating that man can today fulfil himself only in the former.

at the same time as it placed liberty and happiness on the agenda, invented the *ideology* of liberty and happiness, i.e. of two 'essences' which are the precise opposite of their true meaning.[15] Modern man enjoying himself is not really happy, he is playing a part which has been imposed on him without his being aware of it: he is responding to a stereotype.

It will be seen that there is something radical in this conception; the break it entails with the whole left movement of this half-century endows it with a somewhat millenarian, heretical hue. On one point, however, it still seems to exhibit a degree of orthodoxy: the subject of revolution. To the Situationist International, the standard-bearer of the revolution and prime liberating force is still the proletariat. In this respect, there is a major divergence from the theories of H. Marcuse, to whom the proletariat is endowed with no privileged function, quite the reverse.

Let us attempt to specify the leftist conception of the proletariat, which is far from obvious. The difficulty arises from the break with the economist conception of the class struggle. In a cyberneticized society, the proletariat will be 'almost' everybody (since even the 'masters' are themselves programmed),[16] or alternatively, it will compromise all those who are unable to modify the space–time which society allocates for their consumption (the leaders being those who organize that space–time and who themselves have some margin of personal choice in the running of their own lives),[17] or finally it will be represented by the 'historic class swollen to a majority of wage-earners'.[18] Guy Debord, editor of *Internationale situationniste*, is more specific: the modern proletariat, he says, is composed of the 'vast majority' of workers who have lost all chance of working at their own life; it is reinforced by the disappearance of the peasantry and by the

15. Vaneigem, op. cit., p. 44.

16. *Internationale situationniste*, 7 (April 1962), p. 13. Cf. also Th. Frey in No. 10 of March 1966.

17. *Internationale situationniste*, 8 (January 1963), 'Notes éditoriales'.

18. 'Le Commencement d'une époque', in *Internationale situationniste*, 12 (September 1969).

extension of the logic of factory work, which has become applied to a major part of the services and intellectual professions.[19] So defined (or undefined), the proletariat alone would be capable of abolishing class: not because it *is* the proletariat (no 'maturing' of objective conditions will bring about the revolution) but because it alone is able to raise itself to the level of consciousness of its own alienation. In this may be seen the situationists' complete reversal of the conceptions of Lenin or even of the older Marx. A subjective condition is placed in the forefront: the proletariat cannot become *the* power except by *becoming* class-conscious. Lukács stated as much when he wrote that reification 'stamps its imprint upon the whole consciousness of man', and only the proletariat is conscious of its own becoming.[20] It will be possible to surpass everyday life thanks to the violence of this feeling.

The role of the proletariat is certainly a historic role: it has always endeavoured to de-alienate mankind: but it has done so to the advantage of other social classes. In this process, alienation became increasingly burdensome because it became a social alienation in the course of the battle against natural alienation.[21] From that time on, it became for the proletariat a matter of abolishing all alienations.

The dialectic, and the dialectic alone, makes it possible to rise to the level of appreciation of alienations, and in particular of the most powerful of all: the alienation of spectacle. The proletariat is a dialectician, or will become one. Revolutionary theory will therefore not be a scientific system which lays down the law of evolution for all; it will be *understanding* of the struggle: it is this understanding that the revolutionary will endeavour to expand. If this conception lays aside all 'conscious organization' on the Bolshevik model, it also avoids anarchism (although it must be said that traces of anarchist influence are detectable in situationist theory), for it is felt that

19. Guy Debord, *La Société du spectacle*, p. 95.

20. G. Lukács, *History and Class Consciousness* (Merlin Press, 1971), p. 100.

21. R. Vaneigem, 'Banalités de base', in *Internationale situationniste*, 7 (April 1962).

the anarchists are only concerned with the result of the class struggle, not its method; they still allegedly cling to the possibility of economic struggle alone, and counter the State with a negation that is again ideological.[22] To the situationists, who draw their 'total rejection' from the libertarian thinkers, anarchism does not derive its theory from reality but from its own desires: consequently it justifies ideology. So it is upon the proletariat, the subject of the revolution, that the responsibility for the supreme act must fall: the realization of art.[23]

What of youth? It was long thought that leftism after Marcuse reserved an active, if not the priority, part in the revolutionary process to the young. Before May 1968, it may be said that most of the groups of extreme left-wing students, following an old communist tradition, regarded themselves as sections (often indeed as 'trainee units') of an adult party. The young were not recognized as possessing any special role; Marxist analysis even denied them the status of a social group. This was in flagrant contrast to the fact that the greatest activism was to be found among the young, and that opposition to the left establishment was perpetuated primarily among the students. May–June 1968 gave new prestige, notably on an intellectual level, to the role of youth as the *avant-garde* of the revolution. The ideas of H. Marcuse, of American and German dissident students (SDS) produced a climate in which the privileged role of the young in social *contestation* could be accepted.

The university confrontation of the years 1966–8 which preceded and inspired the 'disorders' at the University of Nanterre in April–May 1968, from which the revolt started, was nevertheless founded on analyses extremely unfavourable to the students. At the time of the events which disturbed the academic year 1966–7 and which have become known as the 'Strasbourg

22. G. Debord, op. cit., p. 73.
23. cf. *Internationale situationniste*, 1 (June 1958), 'Notes éditoriales'. During the first period of their activity (1957–62), the situationists saw art as the priority area for the revolution, for it is this very sector which is the most alienated; cf. *Appel aux intellectuels et artistes révolutionnaires*, reproduced in *Internationale situationniste*, 3 (December 1959).

Scandal', the situationists published a text in which they assigned to the student body the sole and unique role of merging with the mass of workers.[24] As for the 'Strasbourg University Scandal', it had been assiduously fanned by the publication of a pamphlet by the local UNEF branch, in fact written by the situationist Mustapha Khayati, entitled: *The Poverty of the Student Condition, considered from the Economic, Political, Psychological, Sexual and, in particular, Intellectual Point of View, with some Measures for Remedying it*.[25] This paints a contemptuous picture of the student as a member of the most alienated of all sociological categories. He is all the more to be despised for the fact that he believes in an independence which is entirely illusory, and elevates his survival to the status of a *way of life*: political false consciousness is found in the pure state in the student. Under these circumstances, he is quite incapable of making, on his own initiative, a critique of the university, of his role in society and of his own alienation. In the same piece, however, Khayati foresees a period of confrontation of which youth 'appears' to be the guiding spirit.[26] To him, however, this is nothing but a sign heralding a forthcoming revolutionary explosion. A major social crisis is felt more acutely by the young. Lefebvre, for his part, shared this point of view: youth, he wrote in 1962, suffers most from the gap between representation and reality, between the possible

24. 'Nos buts et nos méthodes dans le scandale de Strasbourg', in *Internationale situationniste*, 11 (October 1967). At the beginning of the 1966–7 academic year, students favourable to the ideas of the Situationist International got themselves elected to the committee of the local branch of the student union, the UNEF. On the advice of the situationists, they used union funds for the purpose of publishing a number of situationist tracts and pamphlets, and then dissolved their own union branch, arguing in justification that all syndicalism is of the nature of a mystique and bureaucratic to boot. The whole affair is recounted in No. 11 of *Internationale situationniste*.

25. *De la misère en milieu étudiant considérée sous ses aspects économique, politique, psychologique, sexuel et notamment intellectuel et de quelques moyens pour y remédier* (AFGES [Federal Association of Strasbourg Students], first edition, 1966). There were several editions, and translations were made into several foreign languages.

26. AFGES, op. cit., p. 15.

and the impossible; but he, too, denied it the function of 'renewing social life', which is the sole prerogative of the proletariat.[27] The fundamentally non-revolutionary nature of youth, as a sociological category, only holds out hope for overcoming this condition at the most primitive level: skinheads (who reject work but accept goods), provos (who rebel, but fall back into a neo-reformism of everyday life), and, finally, rebellious students who, through the medium of their own condition, call in question the whole of society. But they cannot go further, because the *content* of their subversion is so weak. They can only hand on the torch of dissent to other categories.

By the middle of the nineteen-sixties, if not earlier, the situationists foresaw and predicted the 'second proletarian assault on the class society'.[28] It would present itself in an *illegal* form: anti-trade-union struggle, wildcat strikes, rejection of the old politics, rebellious youth. But the revolution itself, how would it break out, in what form, what would be its content? Here the situationists went much further than any other leftist group of the time, breaking with all *tradition* of revolution and drawing their inspiration from two different sources: the millenarian movement and modern art.[29] All revolutions up to now have been failures. The revolution has to be reinvented. The concept of revolution created by the Situationist International is that of *total contestation* of modern capitalism.[30] This consists of a multitude of spontaneous acts working towards a radical modification of the space–time

27. H. Lefebvre, *Introduction á la modernité* (Paris, 1962), p. 194. Cf. also the twelfth prelude.

28. G. Debord, *La Société du spectacle*, p. 97.

29. The influence of *Socialisme ou Barbarie* on the Situationist International should not be underestimated. By 1954 (*Socialisme ou Barbarie*, 15–16), Chaulieu was writing that modern man needs to liberate himself from all alienations, in particular cultural alienations; that he must refind his lost creativity and capacity for expression.

30. cf. Guy Debord, 'Perspectives de modification consciente de la vie quotidienne', a paper read to the Research Group into Everyday Life set up by H. Lefebvre, reproduced in *Internationale situationniste*, 6 (August 1961). Cf. also No. 8 (January 1963), 'Notes éditoriales'.

imparted by the ruling class. The new revolution thus cannot aspire to the mere seizure of power, a simple renewal of the governing team or of the ruling class: it is power itself which must be suppressed in order to realize art, which is the ultimate objective. The realization of poetry, which at the same time entails superseding it, clearly requires a recognition of one's own desires (stifled by the show society and diminished into pseudo-desires): free speech, true communication (not uni-lateral and manipulated, as now), rejection of productivity for its own sake, rejection of hierarchies, of all authority and of all specialization. The liberated man will cease to be *homo faber* and will become an artist, that is to say the creator of his own works.[31] The revolution will thus be an act of affirmation of the subjectivity of every individual in the cultural field, which is the most vulnerable sector of modern civilization. For it is art which first reveals the extent of the breakdown of values – which Marx and Engels did not see, or did not wish to see;[32] for culture, while it is a reflection of the dominant forces of its time, is also and at the same time a scheme for its own super-session. Great artists have also been great revolutionary prophets: Lautréamont and Rimbaud, for example, who sur-passed their time in and through their work. This thread, since lost (since modern art has become a piece of merchandise like any other), must be found again. A language of communication must be recreated within a community of dialogue: *contesta-tion* will also be a search for such a language, that is why it is to be first of all a *cultural* revolution. Dadaism and surrealism began to destroy the old (alienated) language, but were unable to find a new one to replace it, unable to create a *way of life*. Their failure is explained by the 'immobilization' of the revo-lutionary onslaught during the first quarter of this century. Henceforth it became a question of going beyond art: the surrealists were wrong, says H. Lefebvre, to escape from every-day life into the surreal; the important thing to do is to in-corporate the miraculous into the everyday; before life can

31. cf. *Internationale situationniste*, 12 (September 1969), 'Le Com-mencement d'une époque'.
32. R. Vaneigem, *Traité de savoir-vivre* . . ., p. 185.

become the art of living, art has to invade life. Why assign this central role to art, and to surpassing it in the revolutionary process? Because artistic activity enables participation by the individual in the world: art has always been the highest form of creative work. The individual can only become liberated if art ceases to be a specialized activity, ceases to be, in its mercantile form, a reified activity. To paraphrase the leftists, it may be said that men will only be happy when they are all artists.

Between aesthetic creation and the free (artistic) style of life, a middle ground has to be established by the show society: the work of art as a search for aestheticism. The situationists began their activities of *contestation* (from 1957, and earlier in the *Internationale lettriste*) with an implacable attack on all aestheticism, on all *separate* art. In this activity, they have established a number of techniques: redirection, guerrilla warfare in the mass media, the production of situationist comic-strips and films.[33] But their main weapon remains criticism by the pen: the style they have developed and which has reached a remarkably high level of cohesion has adopted some of the techniques of Hegel and the young Marx, such as inversion of the genitive (weapons of criticism, criticism of weapons), dadaism (a rapid flood of words, words used in senses different from their conventional meaning, etc.). But above all, it is a style permeated by irony.[34] Its critique is aimed relentlessly at all who make no effort to progress beyond the show society; it is particularly hard on the traditional left and its 'thinkers'.[35] The revolution, being a generalized counter-force against everyday life, must, we have said, attack existing art. But it must also oppose all its by-products: architecture, town planning, etc. Liberation of the desires requires total reconstruction of the socio-geographical environment. The situationists have given

33. cf. the article by R. Viénet entitled 'Les Situationnistes et les nouvelles formes d'action contre la politique de l'art' in *Internationale situationniste*, 11 (October 1967).

34. cf. Lefebvre's analysis of irony as a stylistic device that represents a negation of the existing state of affairs: *Introduction à la modernité*, Introduction.

35. Ample illustrations will be found in the pages of *Internationale situationniste*.

some examples of this form of 'redevelopment' in their experiments in unitary town planning, in 'drifting' (free exploration with no itinerary fixed in advance) and even by drawing up plans of buildings and new towns.[36] Cultural activity as a method of experimental reconstruction of everyday life obviously corresponds to a total liberation of man's desires (contrasted with needs and pseudo-needs, which are 'manufactured'), and to an irruption of *subjectivity* on to the stage of history.

This incorporation of the subjective dimension in the revolutionary quest is a completely new phenomenon in the tradition of the labour movement, if we exclude individualist anarchism. Even Henri Lefebvre, who in many ways may be regarded as the main precursor of modern leftism, hardly moves away from the traditional ground of collectivism and social objectivity.[37] In the situationist vision of the revolutionary process, which is supposed to culminate in the realization of the 'whole' man (man reconciled with himself), the struggle of the subjective broadens the front of the old class struggle. The origin of this notion, completely foreign to Marxism (which is the theory of the industrial society, to use G. Lichtheim's phrase), may be sought in the works of the 'poètes maudits' and their successors. Vaneigem recognizes this when he writes that Lautréamont had already said it all[38] and that the ancestry

36. cf. the first five issues of *Internationale situationniste*. 'The proletarian revolution,' writes Debord, 'is also a critique of human geography through which individuals and communities must construct the landscapes and the events which will enable them to take over ... the whole of their own history.' Debord, *La Société du spectacle*, p. 145.

37. Henri Lefebvre's contribution is primarily sociological; a continuing thread of concern for scientific analysis may be traced through all his works (see his *Vie quotidienne dans le monde moderne*, and his work on 'urban revolution'). His revolutionary theory is very backward by comparison with his research work, which in its time was truly *avant-garde*. Despite, or perhaps because of, the criticisms of idealism levelled at him by the CP (since his departure), Lefebvre wants to be regarded as a *Marxist* and nothing but a Marxist. For his influence on the IS (and vice versa) cf. *Internationale situationniste*, 11 (October 1967), in f.

38. 'Banalités de base' (continued) in *Internationale situationniste*, 8 (January 1963).

of the Situationist International may be traced back through de Sade, Fourier, Lewis Carroll, Lautréamont and the surrealists – through all those, in fact, who opened new perspectives to the imagination.

Through the prism of subjectivity, we return to the critique of everyday life, the starting point of the radical critique. Man's subjectivity may find fulfilment in the everyday, not in politics or economics; that is where the most important battlefield is to be found. The exploitation of labour, the only kind considered by Marx, is today included in the wider exploitation of everyday creativity. In this whole area, life has become humdrum, stifling, banal, all passions repressed. But people today want to live. And they perceive the means to that end – the full life *is* the new poetry. And the best and most complete revolution of economic structures could never guarantee the achievement of poetry. Nature must be rediscovered, social relationships rebuilt on the foundations of the everyday. Creativity that is spontaneous will break the bonds of the repressive society. It is as artists and creators that individuals become permeated with radical theory, through the will to create and realize that which is in every one of us. Creativity is revolutionary by its very essence: it is not merely a question of bringing art back to its first inspiration, in everyday life, as some (including Lefebvre) would have it, but of changing the latter.

This design of flooding our day-to-day existence with the light of subjectivity is already contained complete in Rimbaud's 'will to change' life; the 'disordering of all the senses' of the adolescent of Charleville is exactly matched by the 'unchaining of the senses' of the situationists. Both are attempts at breaking down all barriers.

The revolution will be victorious on the day when the conditions for the lasting realization of subjectivity have been created.[39] On the eve of the 'events of May' 1968, the situationists believed that the historic hour was at hand: the hour at which radical subjectivity was to encounter the objective possi-

39. R. Vaneigem: 'Avis aux civilisés relativement à l'autogestion généralisée', in *Internationale situationniste*, 12 (September 1969).

bility of changing the world. They saw on the horizon the prospect of changing the world and 'changing life'. The new era,
the era of the revolution accomplished, was itself described in a
manner if not entirely new, at least very different from the
society of which Lenin and Trotsky dreamed. It was a world
in which the realization of individual liberty would create collective liberty: in this there is no question of some kind of
superiority on the part of the collective, neither in Rousseau's
sense of the general will, nor in the Bolshevik notion of the
proletariat, an entity which had become sanctified. Universal
harmony would reign: between man and his fellows, man and
nature, and man and his own nature – in short, the harmony
of the whole man. Everyday life would be typified by a *reversal
of perspective*: the sum total of individual perspectives harmonized. A reversal because human relationships would no
longer be founded on mediation, conditioning, manipulation,
but on participation, communication, achievement. It would be
the paradisical reign of creativity, spontaneity, pleasure. The
criterion would be qualitative: everybody could become an
artist and all activities would become creative; poetry would
finally become integrated with everyday life.

To describe the new humanity in a few words, it may be said
that it represents the *civilization of play*. All its activities would
be in the nature of a game (in the sense of a spontaneously
accepted, creative activity). The Situationist International con-
tinuously came into conflict with other radical groups, with
which it otherwise had a fairly close affinity (such as *Socialisme
ou Barbarie*, for example), over the problem of work: to the
situationists, emancipation had to come about through the
abolition of work in favour of a 'new type of free activity'.[40]
Productive labour has always been idealized and play under-
valued. The civilization of technology has pushed this tendency
to extremes: it has elevated work to the level of a sacred myth
(both in the East and the West). Man has thus been deflected
from his creative capacity. The new method of dominating

40. *Internationale situationniste*, 8, 'Notes éditoriales'; cf. also No. 1
('Contribution à une définition situationniste du jeu') and No. 4 (the
'Manifesto' quoted above).

nature would be through the creation of an 'atmosphere of play'. The game would be the sole universal value. Automation makes such a prospect possible, and the 'play' form of social organization will compensate for any surviving disagreeable elements in human activity.

The assertion that productive labour is one of the devices used to ensure the maintenance of order, that the imperatives of productivity are nothing more than imperatives of survival,[41] is utterly foreign to the dominant version of socialism that emerged from the nineteenth century: to the Marxists, man creates himself through work, it is simply a matter of liberating him from exploitation; the anarchists retain a quasi-mystical equation of work with moral value, seeing labour as a purifying force, which gives the producer a superiority over the lazy, non-productive capitalist.

It is certain that the situationists, whose aphorism, 'Don't work *ever*!' covered more than one wall during May–June 1968, are the children of their time, that is to say of a society of relative abundance. Their very logic betrays this: what is the good of ensuring your economic survival if you then die of boredom? What is one to do with a nature that is fashioned and deformed by men and classified in terms of profit? The creative activity which they contrast with productive work already belongs to the play era of the future or, as some would say, to utopia. We have seen the direct sources of their inspiration, Lautréamont ('Poetry should be made by all. Not by one.'), de Sade (widening the scope of the desires), and the surrealists. The leftist intention, undoubtedly, is also a quest for the 'whole' man, who, to enrich the concrete nature of his real existence, brings the irrational into his experience.[42] The irrational, as an added dimension, has traditionally been invoked, if not monopolized,

41. Vaneigem goes so far as to cite the semantic origins of the word for work (*Labor*) as signifying punishment, penalty – *Traité de savoir-faire* . . ., p. 52. This represents a return to the utopian socialism of Fourier, whose hypotheses and projections were henceforward adopted by the leftist movement.

42. On Lautréamont's contribution in this field, cf. the preface by J. Gracq to P. Ducasse's edition of his *Works* (published by La Jeune Parque, Paris, 1947).

by *reactionary* thinkers, as an obscure ('natural') justification for the existing state of things. Leftism, in its desire to enrich everyday life, goes back beyond the rationalism and positivism of the eighteenth and nineteenth centuries to the search for the absolute undertaken by the heretical sects of the Middle Ages and the Renaissance, back to feudalism, to the extent that it represents a social order in which the freedom of choice of the individual (of the nobility, needless to say) guarantees the cohesion of the group. Beneath a solid layer of materialism, it attempts to rediscover an epoch before the industrial era when the separation between play and work, between private life and public, professional life had not yet come about. It wants to resuscitate that epoch, to re-establish a still factitious unity in order to surpass it. In this sense, utopia is not intended to serve as an escape-hatch into the unreal, but as a method of exploring the unknown; according to this view, utopia is that impossible possible[43] that will bring about the expansion of the area of the everyday.

The new form of social organization will make it possible to realize poetry, and therefore socialism. On a practical level, socialism will come about thanks to a universal movement towards workers' control. That is to say, the running by the masses of their own lives, in all their aspects: in and through workers' control the proletariat will be able to emerge from its struggle against contemplation; it will become the agent of history.

43. The expression is derived from H. Lefebvre. It should be pointed out that apocalyptic influences are by no means disowned. G. Debord regards millennialism as a modern revolutionary tendency, but one which still speaks the language of religion: Debord, *La Société du spectacle*, p. 116.

4. The theory of council communism

Criticisms of present-day organized communism and of traditional working-class organizations have turned into a renewed critique of the exploitative society (i.e. of all existing socio-economic régimes). This critique has appreciably widened the classical perspective of Marxist analysis. To paraphrase the language of strategy, it may be said that a multiplicity of new fronts have been opened. Economic alienation is not denied: the situation of the producer separated from his product is still seen as *absolute* alienation. At the same time, however, this critique pointed out that the worker was the victim of a multitude of different kinds of alienation in the course of his everyday life, in his daily behaviour and activities. According to this view, the family is a primary alienating structure to the extent that it reproduces the authoritarian and hierarchical model of world society; family socialization already moulds the child's psyche so that he will adapt to the role of operative reserved for him. School and the entire pedagogic tradition continue the work of adapting the child, draining him of his spontaneity, his curiosity, his natural desire to create. All of sexual morality, taboos and prohibitions also tend towards the annihilation of the free individual personality. Once the child grows up, he will have imposed on him the role of consumer, worker, pensioner, etc. In every aspect of his life he will be *separated* both from his desires and their *true* satisfaction.

In order for him to recover his essential humanity, the individual must not simply become conscious of the economic and political reality of alienation; he must abolish separation in every sphere of life by becoming his own master. On the collective level, this means assuming control of every sector of social life. The revolutionary aspirations of leftism quite naturally flow out into *universal workers' control*.

How are these aspirations to be realized? What mode of organization will, or ought, to permit workers' control at every level?

Marxism was embodied by the Party, even in Marx's own lifetime. Marx and Engels did not contest either the need for a party or the need for leadership (even the Communist League had a Central Committee). However, neither Marx nor Engels produced a theory of organization. It was Lenin's theory (set out in its purest form in his *What is to be Done?* of 1902) which provided the most complete version of the Marxist viewpoint on the question of organization. The whole of Lenin's conception is founded on the assertion that the only consciousness acquired spontaneously by the working class is awareness of its economic and corporate interests. In order to acquire a socialist consciousness (i.e. an awareness of the need for revolution), it must rely on those who have a *clear* awareness of historical evolution. According to this notion, the Party thus represents the suitable organism for imparting to that class the consciousness of its own class situation and leading it in the assault on the bourgeois State.

This analysis is the one more or less accepted by all the *extremists*, such differences as there are concerning merely the organization of that organism (flexible or rigid leadership principle, hierarchy, discipline, prohibition or tolerance of factions, etc.) and the question of its relationship with the working class.

Leftism, in contrast, sees the consciousness of the proletariat as itself the factor affecting historical evolution. There is thus no question of a revolutionary party that is the repository of class consciousness. Far from providing the fount of knowledge with which to impregnate the masses, the party organization can only come into being as the *expression* of the spontaneous consciousness of the workers. Leftism confronts *party communism* with *council communism*.

In May–June 1968, the watchword of councils spilled over out of the small circle of theoretical discussion groups. Action committees sprang up like mushrooms: the precise assessment of their actual and potential role gave rise to discussion which still continues to this day. Had the reality overtaken the theory? Council communism, at all events, lies at the heart of leftist theory: the question now is to grasp its real significance through the multifarious conceptions which have been expressed in recent years. For they reflect the doubts and the limitations of the whole movement; beyond the mere matter of organization, the whole idea of socialism is called in question.

The theory of workers' councils may mean one of several different things: historically, it emerged out of reflection on the Soviet revolution and on the failure of the councillist movement in Germany. At that time it was still a tributary of Marxism, and regarded itself as the correct interpretation thereof. It is also concerned with the type of management appropriate to the emancipated society: on this level, it is intended to provide the content of socialism (economic, social and political life managed by the organization of councils). Finally, in a more restricted sense, the theory of councils suggests a model for the revolutionary organization of the proletariat. But two apparently unrelated questions immediately arise here: does this mean the spontaneous organization of the proletariat once the revolutionary process has been set in motion, or the organization of the revolutionary movement as it is supposed to emerge from the day-to-day struggle in a pre-revolutionary situation? Clearly the two questions are closely linked and partisan analysis rarely separates them. The boundary between workers' councils as the content of socialism and workers' councils as organization is itself extremely blurred, and the present separation of the various levels of discussion is completely arbitrary. However, it is through problems of organization that leftism attempts to assert itself, since these are the problems which seem the most urgent and immediate.

It should also be noted that the believers in council communism do not share all the conceptions set out earlier on the critique of everyday life. Council theory is very much older, for a start, than situationist theory. Those who first propagated it in France tended to cling to a critique which was basically economic, if not exclusively so. By contrast, the younger generation adopted the watchword of councils from the start. What is important for our purpose is, in the last analysis, to disentangle the various strands which converge to form a single vision of society and the revolution, to the extent that that vision runs counter to Marxism–Leninism. Before finding a balance that is both coherent and stable (if it ever does), leftist theory has juxtaposed various elements which are frequently apparently heterogeneous. Did not Marx himself postulate the synthesis of the 'three sources': English political economy, French utopian socialism and German philosophy?

In order to understand the meaning of the discussion which surrounds the concept of the 'workers' council', it is necessary to recall the historical tradition, which French leftism has both adopted and overtaken. This tradition has sprung from several different sources. Firstly anarchism, which began in the nineteenth century to systematize the experiments in self-management tried out in the workshops of 'free and independent' craftsmen, and projected the vision of these experiences into an idealized future reproducing a past that was irretrievably lost. Then the revolution of 1905 inspired in Rosa Luxemburg a train of thought which, contrasting with her ultra-orthodox Marxism and her militancy, did not fail to have a profound influence on *three* social-democratic parties. She observed that the revolution, through the length and breadth of the Russian Empire (of that time), was unleashed spontaneously, without any coordination or prior decision being taken, and she deduced from this that it is not in the power of a party either to launch or to prevent a revolution.[1] This obviously immediately poses the problem of the *avant-garde* role of the Party. Rosa Luxemburg goes further still by asserting that not only does the revolutionary organization not provoke the event (in the present instance a general strike), but that the organization is itself the product of the struggle.[2] Certainly in writing this she was not necessarily referring to workers' councils (of which she had,

1. Rosa Luxemburg, *Grève de masses, parti et syndicats* (Paris: Petite collection Maspéro, 1969), pp. 134–5.
2. ibid., p. 146.

n fact, had experience) but to all forms of organization which he proletariat might set up, whether trade unions, parties or works councils. Here in embryo was the hard core of the councillist viewpoint: in the course of its struggle, the proetariat spontaneously creates the organization it needs. To the eftists, this can only be a *non-centralized* form like the works committee or the workers' council. To Rosa Luxemburg, it was not a question of the masses rejecting the Party. In her here was a clear contradiction between the orthodox militant, irmly rooted in her own time and place, and the lucid analyst ble to draw conclusions of universal validity from an isolated event. These two aspects always coexisted in her: her quarrel with Lenin on the subject of the Party, then her critique of the Russian Revolution and finally her lack of enthusiasm for oining the Third International, are all strands of the same hread. Towards the end of her life, she placed all her confidence in the revolutionary instinct of the masses, in particular as manifested in workers' councils such as had appeared in Germany in 1918.[3]

It is true that she continued to work within the framework of he Party, that her works on political economy were scrupuously Marxist and that she participated in all the Party's 'internal' disputes. There is a wealth of material for historical polemic which I shall not go into here. The significant fact is hat the first aspect of the thought of Rosa Luxemburg was aken up by some leftists; for some years there has been a myth of 'Luxemburgism' as a doctrine in its own right. It is certainly he case that Rosa Luxemburg was the initiator of a new radition, and that the new leftism lies within the scope of that radition.

Georg Lukács also exhibited something of the same ambiguity: he was at one and the same time a Party man and a heoretician of the spontaneity of the masses. It has been shown hat he saw class consciousness as the driving force of history, he decisive factor in the self-liberation of the proletariat. Both

3. cf. her speech to the constituent congress of the German Communist arty (in A. and D. Prudhommeaux, *Spartacus et la Commune de erlin* [published by Spartacus, Paris, 1949], p. 55).

an actor and passionately concerned observer in the Russian and Hungarian revolutions of 1919, he did not fail to draw conclusions on the historic role of the proletariat, conscious of the part it had to play and of the tasks before it. When, in March 1920, he considered the problem of how class consciousness could assume concrete form to become a real and effective force, his immediate answer was: by workers' councils. Moreover, his conception was very far-reaching, since the workers' council in his view is a kind of quasi-essence in which all contradictions are resolved, the form in which class consciousness has pursued its struggle ever since its birth.[4] Once again one could conduct a closely reasoned historical exegesis, and demonstrate that the Party organization against which Lukács sets the workers' council is in fact the old reformist social democracy. Nevertheless, his conception was to find in modern leftism a very favourable soil for transplantation.

I have already mentioned the anarchist tradition as one possible medium for the transmission of the councillist tradition. There was no shortage of talk, after the 'events' of May-June 1968, about 'libertarian revolt', a renewal of anarchism, etc. Historians of the labour movement have taken pains to demonstrate the perennial reappearance of anarchist ideas and even the direct influence of anarchy on these events.[5]

The fact that some anarchist ideas were enshrined in the leftist demands, the '*prise de parole*' of spring 1968, is undeniable. They may be found in every period of social unrest, revolt and upheaval. The problem of the perenniality of the anarchist tradition and its influence on leftist theory, however, occurs in quite another form. It is closely dependent on the existence of a libertarian movement, on its liveliness and popularity among the theoreticians of the new revolution.

The anarchist movement itself has been moribund in France since the end of the First World War. The anarchist tradition, for its part, has been kept alive by a small number of talented

4. *History and Class Consciousness* (Merlin Press, 1971), p. 80.
5. cf., for example, D. Guérin: 'Mai, une continuité, un renouveau', in *Le Fait public*, 6 (May 1969); and J. Maitron: 'Anarchisme' in *Le Mouvement social*, 69 (October–December 1969).

writers (the most remarkable of them being Sébastien Faure) who have generally been content to nurse the flame, to preserve the memory of illustrious forebears: Proudhon, Bakunin, Kropotkin. The main body of anarchist ideas has hardly undergone any renewal or addition, except possibly among colonies of émigrés, principally Russians, who brought up new problems in the light of their experience of the Russian, Hungarian or German revolution.[6]

After the war, the Federation of Anarchists (FA) and the Federation of Libertarian Communists (FCL) continued to preach the classic themes in the pages of their newspaper (*Le Libertaire* and later the *Monde libertaire*): in the manner of the orthodox communists, they defended an ideology which they regarded as inviolable, a finished system to be rejected or accepted as a whole. Anarchism was a theorization of a number of rejection symptoms of the budding industrial society. Even taking account of the exaggerations he makes, Marx's critique is far from untrue: in many respects, nineteenth-century anarchism represented a *reactionary* tendency, a utopian desire to return to a vanished society of free and equal artisans. In the face of the concentration of capital and the burgeoning growth of factories, the craftsman and small manufacturer was doomed to disappear.

It remains true, however, that nineteenth-century anarchist thought handed down a number of ideas which were not necessarily dated, such as the frequently clairvoyant critique of Marxism, of the phenomenon of bureaucracy (which Bakunin foresaw with great clarity), of the party and of authority in general, whether exercised by the State, the trade unions or by political parties. But to the extent that the French anarchist movement of the period after the Liberation was unable to renew its theory in the light of the great wealth of experience

6. To be perfectly fair, it should be specified that it is collectivist–anarchist thought which appears to have stagnated. The whole philosophical, ethical and individualistic tradition continues with writers like Émile Armand, C. A. Bontemps, etc. In addition, a number of anarchists devoted themselves to spreading pacifist ideas during the interwar period, the best known of these being Louis Lecoin.

of the previous fifty years, it had become an organization of commemoration (of its great predecessors, great historic date the Spanish legend, etc.).

A second possible explanation for the dissatisfaction of the leftist young may be found in the organizational authoritarianism of the Federation, reinforced by the 'Leninist' experience of Georges Fontenis.

The anarchists' 'shutting out' of the contemporary world was thus balanced by a kind of preservation of the sacred tradition combined with an attitude of extreme hostility towards Marxism in all its forms.[7] It would seem that the deliberate ignorance of the whole theoretical heritage of Marx, Lukács, Korsch further accentuated the isolation of the French anarchist movement and gave it a certain anachronistic air.

It can be asserted without fear of contradiction that 'official anarchism played no part either in recent events or in the emergence of leftist theory.[8] On the other hand, it is none the less true that some isolated groups, cells and individual writers were the vehicles and media for the transmission of those elements of classic anarchism which were susceptible to being absorbed by a more modern theory. These were able to play a role to the extent that they ranged themselves as much against the 'family' of organized anarchism as against Stalinism. The case of the review *Noir et Rouge* is a good example of this. It was read and discussed outside anarchist circles precisely because it refused, in its own words, to engage in the futile exercise of outbidding others in its protestations of anti-Marxism and declared itself ready to receive and study the revolutionary experience of the twentieth century in order to draw such lessons as might be learned from it. The case of *Noir et Rouge*

7. Which led some to take sides with the Western powers against the Soviet *bloc*.

8. This was in fact admitted by one of the moving spirits of the F where declared that this organization had nothing to do with the initiation of the events of May–June 1968 nor played any part in them – interview of Maurice Joyeux in *Le Fait public*, 14 (January 1970). On a purely analytic level, an exception must be made of the 'peri-anarchists' such a B. Péret; cf. G. Munis, B. Péret, *Les Syndicates contre la révolution* (Paris, 1968).

is also exemplary in that the creation of the journal corresponded to the departure of a number of young anarchists from
the FCL on the eve of the 'electoralist' experiment of 1956.
The FCL itself already constituted an attempt at renewal of
the old anarchist Federation; some of the young people who
came into the movement after the war were disillusioned by the
experiment and founded, in November 1955, the Anarchist
Revolutionary Action Groups (GAAR), with *Noir et Rouge*
as their mouthpiece from March 1956.[9] The line taken by *Noir
et Rouge* was to place it outside the existing families, since to
this journal the breach was not between Marxism and anarchism but between a bureaucratic and a libertarian view of
socialism.[10] The journal had certainly come a long way since its
foundation, when the avowed aim of its supporters was simply
to prepare 'the basis of a rejuvenated anarchism';[11] but by
taking a very open-minded attitude, they were immediately
impressed by the modern experiments in workers' councils,
notably in Hungary. From Marxism, *Noir et Rouge* borrowed
the theory of class and the class struggle, and accepted the
importance of its analysis of production relationships.[12]

The positive contribution made by *Noir et Rouge* consisted
in its deliberate policy of not restricting itself to the study of
economic mechanisms, and of adding to the aim of social
transformation the task of revolutionizing the consciousness; in
short, they extended the revolutionary battlefield, culminating
in the assertion that 'The revolution must be total, or not at
all.'[13] But it is clearly the anarchist tradition with regard to

9. For the history of *Noir et Rouge*, see the 46th (and last) issue for an
article by one of its founders, Ch. Lagant: 'Sur le néo-anarchisme'. After
1961 the group itself took the name of 'Noir et Rouge'.

10. cf. the Editorial in Nos. 42–3 of *Noir et Rouge* (November 1968).

11. *Noir et Rouge*, 3, p. 5.

12. ibid., 3, 4 and 28. This very open kind of anarchism should not be
confused with the 'libertarian Marxism' of D. Guérin (*L'Anarchisme*,
Paris, 1965), since in contrast to the latter it refused to accept a complete
synthesis of the two doctrines (cf. No. 28: 'Faire le point').

13. 'La Révolte de la jeunesse', *Noir et Rouge*, 13 (1959). Cf. also No.
11. After 1961, *Noir et Rouge* progressively abandoned the purely ethical
preoccupations of anarchism and established contact with council-
communist groups.

organization that constituted the principal contribution of *Noir et Rouge* to the development of a leftist theory. Initially the paper took up the old anarchist maxim that the means determine the end, in other words that the form of organization in a pre-revolutionary period cannot fail to have an effect on the method of running the socialist society (and hence on the content of socialism), so propagating the classic pattern of organization in small, autonomous groups loosely linked in a voluntary federation. The idea of workers' councils was not altogether absent, but was still referred to only in the abstract.[14] Then, after 1964–5, *Noir et Rouge* brought up and discussed the modern experience of workers' councils, examining the concrete content of this idea as a revolutionary mode of organization and as a method of economic management.[15]

This aspect of the activity of *Noir et Rouge* seems to me extremely important, since it brought to the notice of the reader a whole revolutionary tradition that was practically unknown until the nineteen-sixties, because deliberately ignored by most of the movements that owed allegiance to Marxism. The image of Spanish anarchism propagated by the Party had been one of a counter-revolutionary movement, contrasting sharply with the efficiency of the Marxist parties, the government and the regular Republican Army. In this way, many young militants discovered eye-witness accounts and other texts (for the most part unpublished in France) on the day-to-day operation of agricultural collectives, enterprises run by workers' control, and anarchist bands before they became incorporated in the militias. Similarly, *Noir et Rouge* brought up previously unknown libertarian experiments in self-management: the struggles of the Ukrainian anarchists between 1917 and 1920 (the uprising known under the name of 'Makhnovchtchina', from the name of Nestor Makhno, a

14. cf., for example, *Noir et Rouge*, 4, p. 9, and 10, p. 52, in which the group demonstrated its acceptance of the notion of workers' councils, as then expressed by *Socialisme ou Barbarie* (1958).

15. *Noir et Rouge*, 30 ('Témoignage sur trois collectivités en Espagne'), 31–2 ('L'Autogestion contemporaine' and 'L'Autogestion en Yougoslavie'), 34, 35, 36, 37, 38 ('L'Autogestion en Algérie'), 41 ('Les Conseils en Russie'), etc.

Ukrainian peasant converted to anarchism), and the Kronstadt rising; it also discussed the revolutionary validity of the attempts at workers' control exercised in Yugoslavia and Algeria. In short, without attempting to elaborate a new theory (in which respect it resembled the Situationist International), *Noir et Rouge* was able to break out of the vicious circle of anarchism–Marxism and move on to the road towards possibly superseding this sterile conflict, the road in fact supposedly opened up by council communism.[16]

The historical experience of workers' councils had given rise to some theoretical reflection which, while it was not swallowed whole by French leftism, was the starting point of theoretical research. If journals such as *Noir et Rouge* contributed to our knowledge of the historical experiments in workers' councils, they also facilitated the assimilation of 'councillist' doctrines and their analysis. The most complete of the organizational theories relating to workers' councils is, in fact, based primarily on Soviet and German experience between 1918 and 1921. Leftism, as will be shown later, was to take account of the historical nature of this theory in order to expand it to fit the dimensions of the modern world.

There can be no doubt that it was the German and Dutch far left which drew the most extreme conclusions from the effects of the Russian and German revolutions. Anton Pannekoek (1873–1960) is the most representative thinker of councillist circles. His theory is based on over half a century's experience of militancy. It contained practically all the ideas of the councillists, past and present. It is important to present it here, for all the theoretical discussions and practical activities

16. Daniel Cohn-Bendit, a member of the group, is a good illustration of this 'eclecticism': he defined himself as an anarchist 'negatively', by his rejection of dogmatism, but did not completely reject Marx, any more than he completely accepted Bakunin. When he was pressed to define his position, he placed himself in the general stream of 'council communism' (interview in *Magazine littéraire*, 8 [May 1968]). This state of mind was in fact shared by a number of leftists in May–June 1968. Cf. the author's *Projet révolutionnaire. Éléments d'une sociologie des événements de mai–juin 1968* (Paris, 1969), Chapter 1, 'Les Théoriciens de la spontanéité'.

of the leftist movement were constructed around or stemmed directly from it.

All of Pannekoek's thought is based on three intellectual theses and one historical experience. These theses were formulated before the First World War and they remained central to his thought right up to the end of his life:

1. The materialist view of history. This he clearly derived from Marxism: in studying history and social development, Pannekoek bases his ideas on the relationships between the system of production and the class struggle. In man, the struggle for existence has led to increasingly sophisticated developments in tools. Technical progress, advances in the process of production are crucial to the evolution of the social order. This development itself obeys laws, just like the evolutionary process in the animal kingdom. The agent of this evolution is the class struggle.[17]

2. But this struggle, while it may correspond to changes in the material environment of society (machinery, production, material standard of living), is actually a struggle of *consciousness*. This is the very antithesis of the mechanistic interpretations of a man like Kautsky: the development of material conditions of production cannot hasten the revolution unless they change the workers' consciousness of their material environment. Men have to *think* change before they can accomplish it. The revolutionary process depends both on the development of class consciousness and on the organization of production. It even seems that the subjective element assumed increasing importance in Pannekoek's mind as the years passed: some time before his death he repeated that the aims of this struggle are achieved in the daily experience of the proletarian, by that which is 'alive' in his thought, and also by continual discussion and clarification.[18]

17. There is a continual recurrence of this theme in Pannekoek's writings: see the extracts quoted (in French) by Serge Bricianer in *Pannekoek et les conseils ouvriers* (EDI, Paris, 1969), accompanied by some remarkable explanatory notes.

18. cf. 'Anton Pannekoek's second letter to Pierre Chaulieu', reproduced in *Cahiers du communisme de conseils*, 8 (May 1971).

The proletariat has all the more need for a clear awareness of the tasks it faces because the strength of the bourgeoisie is, today, primarily spiritual. What Pannekoek calls the 'spiritual power of the bourgeoisie' is just as dangerous as its power of material exploitation: [19] bourgeois ideas penetrate the mind of the worker by the logic of the system of production, by education, propaganda, the Church, the press, etc. The proletariat is totally dependent intellectually on the bourgeoisie, and acquiesces in its own enslavement. For it to conquer, it must therefore rid itself of this dependence: capitalism must first be defeated theoretically before being suppressed in practice. 'The road towards liberty will remain closed till the day the working class realizes the importance of independent action and of workers' control.'[20]

3. It is up to the workers as a body to liberate humanity. Pannekoek's view of the revolution and of revolutionary organization flowed from the importance attached to *mass action* in the revolutionary process (a view he had held since before the First World War). It is up to the masses to accomplish 'The Task':[21] they must make themselves masters of their own work, control the means of production. It is therefore also up to them to create the forms of struggle and of organization. Since before 1914 Pannekoek aligned himself with Rosa Luxemburg and other 'radical socialists' in their attempts to develop a theory of the organizational process, in opposition to the practice (and indeed the theory) of social democracy, which had 'institutionalized' the Party once and for all by imposing on it a complex system of central committees, executive bodies, etc. But his 'system' of workers' councils was only to take its final shape after the experience of the revolutions of 1917–20 Russia, Germany, Austria, Hungary).[22] This experience enabled

19. A. Pannekoek, *Workers' Councils* (Melbourne, 1950), p. 29 (published by the 'Southern Advocate for Workers' Councils'). (For a summary, see S. Bricianer, op. cit.)

20. A. Pannekoek, op. cit., p. 230.

21. The title of the first chapter of *Workers' Councils*.

22. In his letter to Chaulieu, quoted above, Pannekoek also says how impressed he was by the political strikes in Belgium in 1893 and in Russia in 1905.

him (negatively) to develop his critique of *party socialism* and (positively) to formulate his concept of *council socialism*.

As early as 1921, Pannekoek was condemning the Russian Revolution as a bourgeois revolution.[23] The régime to which it gave birth, he says, was a State-capitalist régime, to the extent that the bureaucratic class was the exclusive (and collective) owner of the means of production. Like the middle class of the Western countries, it lived from exploitation and from surplus value. But Pannekoek also calls the régime *State socialism*, because the State is the only employer and it also has absolute control of production.[24] Whether State capitalism or State socialism (two aspects of the same reality), the important thing, the reality of the case, is that the proletariat does not control the means of production directly. He concludes from this that party socialism represents a new theory and practice of domination which corresponds to modern capitalism's need for efficiency. Socialism, as a nineteenth-century idea of liberation, was nothing more than the slogan of an imperfect liberation, which proposed to place in power those leaders which the working class had chosen. Its objectives, the nationalization of the economy and the conquest of the State, correspond exactly to the needs of capitalism. 'The [proletariat's] expression of the modest hope for liberation has become the instrument of its voluntary submission to an even worse form of slavery.'[25]

All organizations inspired by party communism have, consequently, become the means either of increasing the power of Russian capitalism, or of taking over the running of free-enterprise capitalism, or again of accommodating itself to the latter. Hence the trade unions now appear as *outside* the working class; they are the intermediaries through which the labour force is put on to the market. They have become an integral part of the 'apparatus of domination', establishment institutions.[26]

23. cf. S. Bricianer's article in *Pannekoek et les conseils ouvriers*, p. 220.
24. Pannekoek, *Workers' Councils*, pp. 201–2 and p. 85.
25. ibid., p. 225.
26. ibid., p. 221.

Anton Pannekoek contrasts party socialism with *council socialism*, which represents the true liberating factor. Pannekoek had the advantage of witnessing such councils in action at the time of the German revolution of 1918–20. But even during the war he had observed the spontaneous formation of works committees with members elected outside (or even in opposition to) the framework of trade-union organization. After 1919, he discussed in various extreme-left-wing journals the merits of the 'Rätesystem'; in it he sensed a possible method of management or even organization of socialist society. Production was to be based on the decisions of a general meeting of the workers on the shop floor. In a large factory, the unit of management would be the shop stewards' committee. Their mandate would be binding, it could be revoked at any time, accounts would be open to universal inspection, wages would be calculated on the basis of the number of hours worked.

Such councils, however, would not be restricted to economic management; they would also provide the political structures to replace present forms of government. Within them, the division between the political and the economic would disappear, as would the division between specialists and producers. The workers' councils would be fully coordinated with one another, horizontally and vertically.[27]

This leads naturally on to a definition of the workers' council in the revolutionary and pre-revolutionary period, and hence to a discussion of *revolutionary organization*. Once again, Pannekoek exhibits here that concern for the concrete so characteristic of him, basing himself entirely on historical examples. The workers' council makes its appearance during a period of revolution; more precisely, it represents the 'new form' of organization forged by the proletariat as a function of the stage of evolution reached by capitalism. Just as the middle class gradually rid itself, in the course of its history, of the masters it had itself set up (municipalities, corporations, princes, monarchs), the working class provides itself with ruling bodies which correspond to the stage of development it has reached. In the workers' council, the proletariat expresses

27. Pannekoek, *Workers' Councils*, Chapter 1.

for the first time its rejection of all new masters: instead of changing its leadership, it abolishes the very function of leadership.[28]

To summarize Pannekoek's thought, it may be said that workers' councils represent, in the first place, a method of political and economic management applied by a socialist society, and in the second place the organ of revolutionary struggle belonging to a given historical phase, namely that in which the working class has progressed to a realization of the tasks facing it. It is difficult to pinpoint the emergence of workers' councils; Pannekoek thinks that the present period brings them into being the moment the struggle reaches a given degree of intensity – which evidently poses the question of the revolutionary process, for councils can only arise in the course of such a process. It is at such moments that the workers become radicalized; a strike committee already contains the seeds of a workers' council.[29] But the revolutionary process itself covers an entire period; this extensive concept clearly contrasts with the notion of revolution as insurrection. What this means is that it is not enough to seize power; the proletariat must, during the preceding period, establish the (spiritual) groundwork for its own accession.

The *autonomous* organizations which the proletariat tends to set up for itself also correspond to new forms of struggle, which are themselves indicative of the level of maturity of the proletariat in the industrialized countries. Henceforth, the struggle against capital takes place by *direct action*. Such action is taken outside the bourgeois forms of opposition (parliamentarianism, ministerialism) and outside the channels of party socialism (trade unionism, party politics). Pannekoek is convinced that as capitalism becomes increasingly brutal and as the proletariat matures, the wildcat strike and the occupation of factories will become its basic weapons: 'They [wildcat strikes] are the precursors of the great struggles of the future, those which will come about when the major social crises

28. 'The Failure of the Working Class', in *Politics*, III, 8 (September 1964), quoted by S. Bricianer, *Pannekoek et les conseils ouvriers*, p. 220.

29. ibid., p. 180.

accompanying social pressures and increasingly violent disturbances drive the masses into ever more vigorous action.'[30]

The problem which Pannekoek poses and which most of the supporters of council communism continue to discuss is that of the existence, the role, indeed the very necessity of a revolutionary organization. In other words, the vexed question of the party arises once again. The author of *Workers' Councils* is far from clear and categorical on this point. He himself oscillates between acceptance of the necessity for organization and a contradictory belief in spontaneity.

Certainly the logic of his system, viz. the spontaneous creation of councils, excludes the possibility of any organization with the specific role of preparing for and, where necessary, sustaining the soviets. This is the idea he is expressing when he says that the proletariat has no need of 'think groups' for its own praxis, for when the time comes it will create its own organs: the councils.[31] It is not the party that creates the revolution, but the class as a whole.

On the other hand, however, it has been shown how insistent he is on the spiritual nature of the process, revolutionary effort being a question of will: men must *think* change before they can accomplish it. Consequently the period of liberation will be one of discussion within the labour movement directed towards choosing 'orientations' for the future.[32] The role of 'think groups' in such discussions would not be a negligible one: they would have to give expression to the ideas that emerged, present them in an acceptable form, and propagate them. In short, they would have the function of establishing the theoretical groundwork.[33]

Pannekoek has been known to be inconsistent on the precise functions of these 'groups'. But throughout his writings he insists on their existence, while specifying that he is not talking about a party in the Leninist sense. He even opposes parties of

30. Pannekoek, *Workers' Councils*, p. 69.

31. ibid., p. 101.

32. ibid.

33. ibid., and 'Prinzip und Taktik' (*Proletarier*, 7 and 8, 1927), quoted by S. Bricianer, *Pannekoek et les conseils ouvriers*, pp. 231–2.

the type of the KAPD (of which he had been a member). Yet the word 'party' is not religiously excluded from Pannekoek's writings. He sees it as a federation of 'working groups', as 'the organ of collective thought', the 'spiritual form' of the proletariat. In 1947, he wrote:

It is [the function] of parties to diffuse ideas and experience, [to] study, discuss, formulate social ideas, and to enlighten the minds of the masses by propaganda. Workers' councils are the organs of practical action, of the struggle of the working class; it is the function of the parties to build up its spiritual strength. Their work is an indispensable part of the auto-emancipation of the working class.[34]

In his letter to P. Chaulieu, quoted above, Pannekoek reproduces almost word for word his idea of the revolutionary party which must enrich the consciousness of the masses so that they may acquire an 'increasingly wide' and clearer awareness of their tasks.

In point of fact, the problem of party organization is treated by Anton Pannekoek in a highly ambiguous manner, if he is to be taken literally: having said that the problem exists, he immediately empties it of all real significance, since it is the masses who, in the last resort, will decide on their own actions. At the same time, however, the 'spiritual' element is of the greatest importance, since the revolution is 'the accession of the mass of the people to the consciousness of their existence and their nature'.[35] In these circumstances the party, defined as the whole body of 'those who see furthest',[36] surely has a crucial part to play. And does this not imply a return to the notion of a party of leadership? The communists, say Pannekoek, are the people with the clearest ideas, the most capable of putting them

34. 'Cinq thèses sur la lutte de classe', French version in *Informations et correspondance ouvrières*, supplement to No. 72 (June–July 1968).

35. Letter written by Anton Pannekoek on 8 November 1953, addressed to Pierre Chaulieu and reproduced in *Socialisme ou Barbarie*, 14 (April–June 1954). (This was the first letter, the only one published in *Socialisme ou Barbarie*.)

36. Quoted in S. Bricianer, *Pannekoek et les conseils ouvriers*, p. 232.

across, and of proposing the best practical measures.[37] But are those very people not the most powerfully motivated to lead and direct the masses? From 'proposing' measures to 'imposing' them is but a short step.

Certainly the ambiguity is there. However, it is not necessarily essential to take Pannekoek literally. The kind of revolutionary organization he is talking about is the type in which he himself was a militant: a working group dedicated to theoretical study and development, with no fixed, immutable structure, which could indeed easily be mistaken for a body like the Groep van Internationale Communisten (GIC) that contained a number of Dutch 'councillists'. In fact, names are of little importance to him: it is the reality of the leadership-oriented revolutionary party that he rejects.[38] In order to understand his idea of organization, it is necessary to enter into the *spirit* of his system. To him, the proletarian revolution breaks out once the proletariat has become aware of its task: if a party takes over the workers' councils and imposes a line of action on them, it means that the class is not yet sufficiently mature. He points out that this is what happened in the Russian Revolution of 1917: the soviets set themselves up spontaneously, and yet the Bolshevik Party took power. This meant, Pannekoek concludes, that it was really 'obliged' to take power, in the sense that the proletariat was incapable of doing so itself, since circumstances were not ripe for a 'true' proletarian revolution.[39]

If we now consider the legacy left by Pannekoek to the proponents of council communism, it must be recognized that some theoretical problems remained unsolved.

For one thing, Anton Pannekoek never lost the traces of his long sojourn in social democracy or of his militant's theoretical

37. ibid.

38. He says as much himself, in fact: 'The name is unimportant, as long as these parties adopt *a role completely different* from that which present-day parties aspire to play.' (Quoted by S. Bricianer, loc. cit., p. 262. My italics.)

39. A. Pannekoek's second letter to P. Chaulieu, *Socialisme ou Barbarie*, 14.

training. He remained a Marxist all his life.[40] Consequently his council communism retained the marks of these origins. In particular, he lays special emphasis on the economic aspects of the class struggle, on the development of economic forces and forms. His historical materialism sometimes spills over into evolutionism (cf. his book *Marxismus und Darwinismus* and also *Lénine philosophe*) and leads him to imagine socialist society as 'productivist' – a society in which work will finally be carried out joyfully. As we have seen, these preoccupations are a considerable distance from more recent viewpoints, such as the analyses contained in the critique of everyday life. It is quite certain that Pannekoek's notions on work are diametrically opposed to those which had their origins in surrealism. His attitude borders on the moral notion of work as having some kind of regenerative power, on the lines sketched out by Marx (man in fashioning nature *fashions himself*), or even Proudhon (work is what confers dignity on man; only the productive worker is worthy of esteem). Similarly, his socialism is in parts quite close to the socialism of Lenin. In a socialist society, he says, the rate of growth and economic progress will reach levels unheard of in capitalist society.[41] His socialism remains impregnated with a positivism which many leftists reject. There is plenty of room for dispute here, and dispute has ensued, as will be seen. In addition, some present-day councillist groups vigorously reject the arguments of the critique of everyday life, exalting militancy at the 'point of production'. This brings us to the question of defining the proletariat: here again, Pannekoek remained a prisoner of his time, holding a very restrictive concept of the proletarian. His vision of the worker possibly excludes today's technician or worker in the tertiary sector.

It nevertheless remains true that in other areas he was able to put across astonishingly modern, even prophetic ideas. Mention has already been made of what he said, as long ago as

40. A fact which is further emphasized by his disciple Paul Mattick in an article dedicated to Anton Pannekoek, written after the latter's death: 'Anton Pannekoek', *La Révolution prolétarienne*, 472 (1962).

41. Pannekoek, *Workers' Councils*, pp. 58 and 59.

1947, about direct action, wildcat strikes, factory sit-ins. Likewise the importance he attaches to the subjective factor (consciousness, will, etc.) is in complete harmony with certain modern leftist attitudes.

Above all, Pannekoek is 'contemporary' because he tried to draft the best formula for putting into effect the maxim that 'the emancipation of the workers must be achieved by the workers themselves'. This is the reason why this theory is at the centre of the current debates on the left: the leftist movements of today are all endeavouring to define their respective positions in relation to it – and also, be it said, in relation to its ambiguities.

THE INHERITORS

The heritage, as we have seen, was that provided by 'autonomist' conceptions of the revolution and of the running of socialist society. It was also embodied by the conception of the organization process as developed by Rosa Luxemburg, Anton Pannekoek and the propagandists of a form of neo-anarchism. Finally, it represents the whole of that historical experience 'discovered' through leftist journals and pamphlets.

How was this inheritance received and interpreted by its legatees? This depended, in the first place, on the particular background and history of each separate group; secondly, on the particular interpretation placed on social realities; and finally, to some it was a question of projecting into the future the theoretical and practical store of experience of the past half century: to these groups, the important thing was to synthesize and innovate, in short to give free reign to the theoretical imagination.

It has been shown that the theory of councils related both to the content of socialism and to what have come to be called 'organizational' problems. It is indubitable that to many leftists this last preoccupation became an urgent one, especially after 1968. We shall therefore pursue the discussion within the ranks of the leftists through the medium of the various theories of organization, while remembering that the question of ends and means cannot be so conveniently compartmentalized.

Two extreme 'poles' may be discerned in this respect: on the one hand there is the 'organizational pole', which while it declares itself in favour of the introduction of councils, does not disguise its attachment to the existence of a party. Then at the other end of the spectrum, there is the 'spontaneist pole' which rejects absolutely all pre-conceived and pre-established forms of organization. Between the two poles, there are a number of intermediate currents which at once reflect different shades of practical experience and different projections.

The organizational conception of P. Chaulieu, who is at the one extreme of the leftist movement, is fairly closely related to that of Lenin. What separates them is Chaulieu's analysis of capitalism, socialism, and their course of development. In this sense, his organizational model supposedly applies to a completely different reality.

Chaulieu asserts that the fundamental division in the capitalist system is not that between capitalists and proletarians, between those who own wealth and those who have nothing to sell but their labour; the decisive division today is between those who give orders and those who carry them out. This *imposed* separation between productive functions is the one that must be abolished. The abolition of private property is a necessary but not a sufficient condition for the advent of socialism. In the Soviet Union, for example, exploitation continues, the division into classes is still a reality. In that country, the separation between executives and operatives, rulers and ruled, far from having disappeared, has actually been reinforced. Therefore socialism means the end of this separation: the management of production will, in the socialist society, be organized on a *collective* basis. On these premises, the organization of socialist society hardly differs in principle from Pannekoek's vision. The workers' council will be the principal organ of political, social and economic administration. Where Chaulieu diverges from Pannekoek is in the design of the precise shape of socialist society, which he describes with a wealth of detail that leaves nothing to chance. He foresees a central assembly, a government of councils, workers' councils at the shop-floor level, their precise coordination and, to crown the economic edifice, a *planning factory* with the task of planning, coordinating and managing the economy at national level.[1] This attention to detail in his projection arises from Chaulieu's view of the modern economy: complex, diversified, requiring centralized direction and control.

Whatever the truth may be about such an emphasis on planning, this kind of socialism differs from Lenin's, according to Chaulieu, to the extent that the proletariat will run its own affairs through the medium of its own organs, democratically elected, removable, etc. No provision is made for a party separate from the masses, playing the part of an *external* leadership. The organizational pattern is also dictated by this consideration. Chaulieu thinks that the revolution can only be made by the workers themselves, with workers' councils being set up in the initial stages. Therein lies, in his view, the crucial divergence from the Trotskyist or Leninist view: it is not the party, a separate formation, but the workers' councils who will be the architects of freedom for the workers. However, Chaulieu adds, in the pre-revolutionary period and on the very threshold of the revolution some central *revolutionary organization* will be essential. Once the revolution has begun, it will be necessary to protect the organization of the councils against possible 'take-overs' by Leninist parties, for the struggle within autonomous organizations would be 'bitter'. The organization of revolutionaries will have to fight to ensure that the councillist viewpoint prevails.[2]

This *revolutionary organization* (which is not yet in existence) is seen by Chaulieu as an *avant-garde*, the organization of a 'conscious minority', which could only be a fraction of the class, and distinct from the class itself. For in a non-revolutionary

1. P. Chaulieu: 'Sur le contenu du socialisme', in *Socialisme ou Barbarie*, 22 (July–September 1957). Cf. also the basic text, *Socialisme ou Barbarie*, in particular section II: 'Bureaucratie et prolétariat', in No. 1 of March–April 1949.

2. 'Réponse au camarade Pannekoek', by P. Chaulieu, *Socialisme ou Barbarie*, 14 (April–June 1954).

period the proletariat is not and cannot be its own leadership The *avant-garde* would be made up of revolutionary intellectuals and of workers; it would itself determine its own organizational structure. But Chaulieu does not hide the fact that a certain degree of centralization will be necessary.[3] The new organization, which will be a 'fusion of the experience of the working class and the positive elements in modern culture,'[4] will set itself a certain number of aims which will be designed to make the class more conscious (in particular of the level of consciousness it has reached), and better able to form a general conception of the problems of society and of socialism. Consequently, the revolutionary organization will have to propagate the notion of workers' councils, while making sure it develops an ideology and defines a programme in advance, so as to supply the working class with the means of self-expression. To this end, the organization will decide on the orientation and the methods of action of the class, and endeavour to get them adopted by 'ideological struggle and example'.[5] Finally, the *avant-garde* will help the workers to protect their immediate interests.

If one examines it closely, the 'universal, minority, selective and centralized' body[6] bears a certain resemblance to the Bolshevik type of party. Chaulieu defends himself against this charge by introducing a distinction which is, in his eyes, of capital importance. The party model he puts forward first of all is set up in support of a self-governing concept of society, and secondly is not a bureaucratic organization; it is not capable of setting itself up as a *ruling* body. All organizations have hitherto degenerated into bureaucratic parties because they all reproduced the fundamental relationship of capitalism : the director/operative relationship. In its struggle, which is also a struggle against bureaucracy (which has penetrated the State,

3. 'Bilan, perspectives, tâches' (unsigned editorial presumably by P. Chaulieu), *Socialisme ou Barbarie*, 21 (March–May 1957).

4. 'Prolétariat et organisation', by P. Cardan (a pseudonym of Chaulieu's) in *Socialisme ou Barbarie*, 27 (April–May 1959), p. 77.

5. P. Chaulieu : 'Discussion sur le problème du parti révolutionnaire', *Socialisme ou Barbarie*, 10 (July–August 1952).

6. ibid., p. 16.

industry and labour organizations), the proletariat will create for itself an organization which will specifically not reproduce this relationship.[7] It will be based on an anti-bureaucratic ideology.

In this form, Chaulieu's conception in the matter of organization has not failed to provoke powerful opposition within the leftist movement, and even within the ranks of his own group, Socialisme ou Barbarie. The objection has been raised, among others, that it is idealistic to suppose, in advance, that at the moment when councils appear the revolutionary organization will dissolve itself to merge with the autonomous organizations so created.[8] Chaulieu has also been accused of trying to crystallize, in an authoritarian manner, the modes of social organization, struggle and propaganda. Finally, it is certain that Chaulieu and his friends, when they spoke of the '*avant-garde*', were thinking of their own group, and that they regarded it as the 'nucleus' of the future party.[9] This is entirely in keeping with the tradition of the Trotskyist groups from which Socialisme ou Barbarie had originally sprung.

Chaulieu's conception, however 'Leninist' it may have been, clearly marked itself off from the Bolshevik tradition, if only by breaking with the *traditional* idea of the party and by advancing class autonomy and spontaneous organization in the form of the workers' council. In addition, it had the merit, at the time it was first expressed, of arousing discussion *within the framework* of the councillist theory itself. This discussion took place, initially, inside the group, and brought about the departure of the 'minority' faction. It is this minority view of organization that must now be examined, for it is diametrically opposed to the previous one: it expresses the 'spontaneist'

---

7. P. Cardan, 'Prolétariat et organisation', *Socialisme ou Barbarie*, 27 (April–May 1959).

8. Theo Massen (an activist in the Dutch 'Spartacus' group): open letter to Chaulieu in No. 18 of *Socialisme ou Barbarie* (January–March 1956).

9. In fact P. Chaulieu never disguised the fact that he reserved for his own group 'a privileged role in the constitution of the *avant-garde*'; see 'Discussion sur le problème du parti révolutionnaire', *Socialisme ou Barbarie*, 10 (July–August 1952).

viewpoint and has had considerable influence on the whole 'spontaneist' wing of the leftist movement.

The most perfect expression of this viewpoint is contained in the writings of Claude Lefort, who campaigned for it within the Socialisme ou Barbarie group on many occasions. Lefort considers that all parties, of every kind, constitute a form of leadership, regardless of the principles of their internal organization. To him, the counter-revolutionary position of the CPSU after 1917 consisted in the very fact of its existence as a party, and not in its 'centralism'. Moreover, he considers that the party is the product of a bygone age in the history of the proletariat, a stage when it expressed the weakness and subjugation of the class. It corresponded to the latter's modest estimation of its own revolutionary powers. Unable to carry out the revolution itself, it placed the burden of this task on to a group that was external to itself.[10] Lefort thus introduces a concept of proletarian history that is far removed from the objectivism of Marxist writers. The historically important factor is working-class awareness of its own struggle and objectives. The greater this level of awareness, the less inclined the proletariat will be to entrust the task of liberation to *external* forces. But where Lefort parts company completely with Chaulieu is in doubting that this consciousness can be aroused or transmitted from the outside. The proletariat's consciousness results from its experience of its own development and the struggles it has fought. Thus Lenin's socialist consciousness was entirely abstract, its content determined by elements foreign to the working class, and of which it had had no practical experience. Nobody can solve the proletariat's problems for it: if it does not find the answers to problems of organization and programme, the reason is that it is insufficiently mature to be able to do so. The question of the class's ability to run society is one which Marx underestimated, even ignored. It is a 'subjective' element, to which Lefort attaches the greatest importance. He considers that the behaviour of the proletariat is not solely the result of its living conditions, any

10. C. Montal (pseudonym of Lefort's): 'Discussion sur le problème du parti révolutionnaire', *Socialisme ou Barbarie*, 10 (July–August 1952).

more than economics can be separated from politics for that class (unlike the case of the bourgeoisie): changes take place because conditions demand that they take place. In other words, politics is not an abstract knowledge of events, but a reality resulting from its day-to-day experience, 'such as is engraved, at least as a tendency, on the life and behaviour of the workers'.[11]

If the party is condemned as attempting to introduce consciousness 'from outside', there is still no question of rejecting every form of organization. While it is true that the proletariat does not acquire an awareness of the universal tasks of the revolution until it actually accomplishes those tasks itself, it is perfectly conceivable that organizations might exist to propagandize the economic benefits of these objectives. Claude Lefort is thus posing the problem of activism, and in doing so he sets himself apart from the extreme wing of spontaneism on the question of organization. The idea of autonomy of struggle, he writes, may be sustained and propagated both by *groups of enterprises* and by groups united on a *purely ideological basis*. These latter groups, which will also include intellectuals, would formulate the revolutionary scope of the battle in progress; supporting, amplifying and clarifying the struggles carried out by the militants in the factories. But it is not their function to develop an ideology, since it is the spontaneous actions of the workers which alone contain, 'in the highest degree', the proletarian ideology, that is to say the rationalization of their own practice.[12] In these conditions, the programme of the *avant-garde* must be to ensure leadership of the working class by itself. The *avant-garde*, that 'provisional, purely *ad hoc* detachment of the proletariat', will have to dissolve itself in the 'representative power' of the class. This power may be constituted by the workers' council, but Lefort, in contrast to Chaulieu, is careful to avoid defining in advance the structures which the class will create for itself.

11. Cl. Lefort, 'Organisation et parti', *Socialisme ou Barbarie*, 26 November–December 1958).

12. 'L'Expérience prolétarienne', unsigned editorial by Lefort in *Socialisme ou Barbarie*, 11 (November–December 1952).

While these two systems represent, broadly, the two pole around which the various leftist groups have tended to as semble, there is no lack of intermediate positions, and ever some more 'extreme'. It is impossible to enumerate them, le alone analyse them all. I shall confine myself therefore to men tioning a few of them, which have the advantage of being immediate, whereas the internal debate within Socialisme ou Barbarie is today of largely historical interest.

The problem which provides the chief bone of contention of leftist theory, that of organization, interests the movement from various angles, but basically it is the conception of *militancy* which needs to be formulated, and secondly the degree of independent *awareness* on the part of the proletariat that need to be brought out.

The first point hardly requires further elucidation: the various aspects of militancy have always been in the forefront of the preoccupations of any leftist group, especially since 1968 The second point, that of the consciousness of the proletariat is important because it touches both the question of organ ization and that of the meaning of the historical process. Both are intimately linked. If it is thought that the working class is capable of a large 'dose' of class consciousness then there is less need to insist on the *avant-garde*. On the other hand, if the proletariat is thought to be incapable of freeing itself from the material and moral strait-jacket imposed on it by the system then there would be more tendency to emphasize the import ance of an organization able to help the workers to throw of their chains.

Hence the two conceptions reflect one another, in principle Some groups have been able to deal with the two problem independently, which has tended to render their system of thought somewhat incoherent.

Of the groups closest to Chaulieu, the first to be considered is the 'Workers' Power' group ('Pouvoir ouvrier'). This came into being as a result of a split in Socialisme ou Barbarie in 1963, due in fact to a dispute entirely unrelated to the ques tion of organization.[13] *Pouvoir ouvrier* was a journal founded

13. Those who left accused Chaulieu of having broken with his own

y the Socialisme ou Barbarie group, aimed at workers on the
hop floor. From that time on, it was to propagate views re-
ating to questions of programme and theory that borrowed
eavily from P. Chaulieu's articles of the nineteen-fifties.[14]
ouvoir ouvrier remains in favour of the power of 'elected and
eplaceable' workers' councils; but holding the view that the
aditional organizations had abandoned the struggle to achieve
iis object, it declared that the group was going to fight to
onstruct the new revolutionary organization that was lack-
ig.[15] This would be fundamentally traditional and classical in
tyle, combining an *avant-garde* of manual workers and intel-
ectuals with the object of 'helping' the workers to realize their
wn destiny. A group performing the functions of orientation,
oordination and struggle, the party is indispensable 'to ensure
iat the struggle of the proletariat results ... in the establish-
ient of working-class power'.[16]

The group does not hide its predilection for centralism as a
rinciple of organization and favours tactics of 'infiltration'
vhich place it fairly close to Trotskyist groups. It even seems
iat, by comparison with the views of Socialisme ou Barbarie,
ouvoir ouvrier has developed towards a more Leninist stance,
vhich places it at the extreme end of the spectrum of the leftist
iovement.[17]

---

aditional analysis of capitalism, in particular in underestimating econ-
mic alienation. It does seem, in fact, that in 1961–2 Chaulieu adopted
ome of the ideas of Marcuse and the situationists.

14. Those who remained in Socialisme ou Barbarie subsequently ac-
ised the dissidents of Pouvoir ouvrier of 'conservatism', to the extent
iat the latter had not accepted the group's theoretical innovations. Cf.
ie circular issued by Socialisme ou Barbarie on 28 October 1963,
nnouncing the split.

15. 'Pourquoi nous luttons', a proclamation reproduced on the back of
ouvoir ouvrier.

16. 'Plate-forme politique de Pouvoir ouvrier', *Pouvoir ouvrier*, 90
May 1968 – printed edition).

17. On the group's participation in trade-union activity, cf., for example,
No. 59 of April 1964, p. 4. After May–June 1968 Pouvoir ouvrier, like
nost of the extremist groups, directed its energies towards the construc-
on of an *avant-garde* organization; cf. the article: 'Peut-on former
naintenant le parti révolutionnaire?', *Pouvoir ouvrier*, 93 (October 1968).

Situationist groups and those inspired by the situationis
philosophy occupy an intermediate position on this spectrum
In its early days, the Situationist International regarded itsel
as a restricted group, having the object of developing theory
In imitation of surrealist practice, the group vigorousl
wielded the weapon of exclusion. Above all, it was importan
to it to preserve intellectual homogeneity among its member
so that the radical critique of society would preserve a degre
of cohesion. In other words, the Situationist International di
not regard itself as a 'revolutionary organization', nor did i
yet raise, on a historical level, the question of the mass imple
mentation of the critique of everyday life. The political vehic
of the radical critique had not yet been identified organiza
tionally. In this field, the situationists were oddly orthodo
holding to a kind of Marxism tinged with Trotskyism. In a
probability their political development (in the narrowest sens
of the word) took place in contact with the Socialisme ou Bai
barie group.[18] However that may be, it is true that from 196
onwards, the Situationist International attached itself to 'th
most radical current', that which campaigned under the sloga
of 'workers' councils'.[19] Over the years, the profile of the 'ne
organization' became more clearly defined: first and foremos
the councils were not intended merely to change the juridica
form of private property or the social origins of society
leaders, but to clear the way for the new revolution. At tha
time,[20] the conception of organization tended to waver som
what, since the situationists considered that the new organiza
tion could only achieve its ends by abolishing itself, its rol
being rather that of a detonator. Did the question of counci
already arise? Or merely of a pre-councillist movement?
is at all events the case that from 1963, the Internation

18. A joint text was drawn up which was to provide a platform fo
discussion in the IS: G. E. Debord and P. Canjuers: 'Préliminaires po
une définition de l'unité du programme révolutionnaire', a tract publishe
on 20 July 1960. For vague references to Marx, see A. Frankin
'Esquisses programmatiques', in No. 4 of *Internationale situationnis*
(June 1960).

19. 'Notes éditoriales', *Internationale situationniste*, 6 (August 1961).

20. ibid., No. 8 (January 1963), pp. 13 and 28.

ecommended the formation of a revolutionary movement which would disappear on the outbreak of the revolution, since the 'free explosion' should not be monopolized by any centre.

In the course of the nineteen-sixties, the IS ended up by identifying the content of socialism with the realization of the aims of the critique of everyday life, and the latter's *conscious* transformation. The proletariat will be able to realize art by generalized workers' control: workers' control meaning control of the whole of society (and not merely of the political and economic sectors).[21] It clarified to some extent its conception of councils by basing itself on the historical experience in the course of which these had appeared. The *present* revolutionary organization should include all those organizations which pursue 'in a consequential manner' the realization at international level of absolute power to the workers' councils.

Internally, this organization must not reproduce 'the hierarchical conditions of the dominant world' and the limits of total democracy will only be defined by the acceptance by all its members of the coherence of its critique. Its aim should be, finally, to disappear as a *separate* organization the moment the councils make their appearance.[22]

On the eve of May 1968, the Situationist International had reached the point of recommending the establishment of a revolutionary organization. By April 1968, Guy Debord was proposing that the International shed its skin, and move from the construction of theories to the stage of 'communication'. Foreseeing revolutionary events 'in the streets', Debord invited his friends to enlarge the circle of supporters so that they would be in a position to embark upon a revolutionary praxis.[23]

In the course of the 'events' of May–June 1968, the situationists were given the opportunity of applying their ideas, both

21. 'Adresse aux révolutionnaires d'Algérie et de tous les pays', in *Internationale situationniste*, 10 (March 1966).
22. cf. the 'Définition minimum des organisations révolutionnaires' adopted by the seventh conference of the IS (July 1966); *Internationale situationniste*, 11 (October 1967), pp. 54–5.
23. G. Debord: 'La question de l'organisation pour l'IS' (April 1968), reproduced in No. 12 of *Internationale situationniste* (September 1969).

on fundamental issues and on the question of organization initially in the first occupation committee for the Sorbonne, and subsequently in the committee for maintaining the sit-in (CMDO). Their point of view was to be confirmed, firstly in their conceptions of workers' councils, establishing workers' control in every field and constituting the new type of social organization which was to put an end to the proletarianization of all. It was also an opportunity for the permanent achievement of subjectivity, which would not be limited to factory workers (with the inclusion of 'workers' wives, people from the area, and volunteers').[24] Secondly, the question of the need for a revolutionary organization in a pre-revolutionary situation was raised: the formation of 'councillist organizations' was proposed. For the situationists were intent on opposing a 'quasi-anarchist spontaneism', the stirrings of which they thought they detected after May 1968. Councillist organizations were to develop a unitary critique of the dominant society and reject the separation of politics from economics (as all 'councillist' organizations had done in the past). Whereas they were neither supposed to constitute a general staff that would produce councils 'to order', nor to express a councillist *ideology*, a kind of *councillism* that could produce ready-made answers, councillist organizations would nevertheless certainly be set up, and the presence of 'conscious' councillists in the future councils would only increase the latter's chances of survival. The councillist theory would be indispensable if the workers' councils were to last.[25]

Within the councils, the councillists would act individually to combat and denounce the presence of any bureaucrats who might infiltrate them. They would also have to guard against 'phoney' or 'reactionary' councils (councils of policemen, for example). In short, the councillists would be the guardians of revolutionary purity. Their struggle was to aim at the abolition of all power external to the councils themselves. No details are

24. R. Vaneigem: 'Avis aux civilisés relativement à l'autogestion généralisée', in *Internationale situationniste*, 12.

25. René Riesel: 'Préliminaires sur les conseils et l'organisation conseilliste', ibid.; cf. also Vaneigem's article, quoted above.

iven as to their composition, except to state that any councilist organization would of necessity consist of at least two
thirds workers.[26]

All in all, specifications as to actual councillist organization
are kept to a minimum: total democracy within it, majority of
the membership workers, councillist programme, but only in
principle since the cohesion of the council would be defined
objectively by the *practical exigencies* of its revolutionary task.
Only historical practice will indicate the precise organizational
forms and the programmatic content of the councils. The
revolutionaries, on the other hand, will have the function, as
from now, of formulating the fundamental principles of
councillist organizations.

This is a kind of middle course, in relation to the two poles
defined earlier: the form and content of the workers' councils
are not specified in advance, the present revolutionary organization is not supposed to resemble a real party. This programme has been followed or imitated by several groups inspired by situationist ideas or close to the IS in their theoretical
approach. The tendency after May–June 1968 was to return to
the concept of a Revolutionary Councillist Organization
(ORC) or a Councillist International. The way was prepared by
the theoretical and practical efforts of autonomous groups, who
did not, however, emerge fully formed, but were born of the
need for struggle and created as the expression of that need.[27]
The very praxis of the group (total democracy, free theoretical
discussion, etc.) was to highlight the positive aspects of the
workers' council. In this sense the group constituted, by its very
existence, an initial exemplary action programme. The ORC is
supposed to go beyond what was actually ever experienced in
the way of workers' councils, particularly in Germany, in that
it constitutes the point at which the total unification of revolutionary praxis will be achieved (non-separation of the
diverse functions of de-alienation), for the proletariat's ability
to lead the revolution itself cannot be resolved into a technical

26. ibid. The council is composed of the 'grass roots', not of delegates.
27. cf., for instance, the programme of one such group: *Pour
l'organisation conseilliste*, 1 (June 1970), p. 18.

ability to direct production.[28] The motivation lying at the roo
of this 'organizational voluntarism' is a refusal to 'wait, as i
for the Messiah, for councils to form themselves'; the duty o
the revolutionary is to fight for their formation, in line with th
current movement of history. The only criterion of revolu
tionary authenticity for an autonomous group will be th
degree of congruence between its critical theory and its prac
tice.

This said, attempts at organization nevertheless actuall
come out as precise and obligatory schematic designs: mos
such initiatives start from the assumption that the theoretica
groundwork has been done and that it is time to emerge from
'contemplation'.[29] They likewise end up with notions which ar
not intended to limit the activity of the group to the mer
provision of information, but demand that the organizatio
intervene as an organization, while still retaining the objectiv
not of seizing and exercising power, but of struggling t
further the seizure and exercise of power by the whole workin
class. The proponents of the organizational models quoted d
not consider the revolutionary organization as either the 'con
science' of the proletariat, nor as its general staff nor, finally, a
its representative. Its role is intended to consist in contributin
to the auto-organization of the class through the 'developmen
and diffusion of revolutionary theory and day-to-day participa
tion in the class struggle'.[30]

The last category of groups favourable to council com
munism is that most closely wedded to spontaneist ideas. Her

28. ibid., p. 23.

29. 'Thèses provisoires pour la constitution d'une Internationale con
seilliste', in *Conseilliste*, No. 0 (April–May 1970). Cf. in the same issu
the organizational principles of the projected Councillist Internationa
pp. 38–40.

30. *Révolution internationale*, 3 (December 1969), p. 36. For
situationist-inspired attempt at 'councillist' organization, read the *Con
tribution à la prise de conscience d'une class qui sera la dernière* (*Contri
bution to the Awakening to Consciousness of a Class which will be th
Last*), published by a 'Councillist revolutionary agitation group for th
formation of the Councillist Revolutionary Organization' (Paris, Januar
1970).

again, there are discernible nuances of difference, relating to the level of revolutionary consciousness attributed to the proletariat. To these groups, all organization is useless and even mischievous, to the extent that consciousness cannot be introduced from the outside. The only reality accepted and supported is one of groups formed spontaneously at the place of work, notably at times of industrial or political action. But to some, the workers' struggle does not necessarily carry with it a sufficient consciousness – this must exist *before* the appearance of workers' councils. This tendency, which may be termed 'ethical', looks upon the revolution as something of a moral duty that it is incumbent upon the proletariat to perform. The proletariat may bring it about, or it may 'betray' it. Workers' councils, which express the revolutionary consciousness of the class, must, if socialism is to be realized, first accept the *socialist ethic*.[31]

This acceptance is not a passive, but a deliberate and voluntary thing. The revolutionary act requires a *revolutionary will*. This will and consciousness are not capable of being 'transmitted'; nor can any *avant-garde* or organization substitute itself for the workers.[32] It is true that the process of this coming to awareness, this awakening of consciousness, is unclear the moment it ceases to be related to the development of economic factors (forces and relationships of production). The objection has been raised within the council socialism group, and the question has been asked: 'How can the proletariat

31. *Cahiers de discussion pour le socialisme de conseils*, 3 (October 1963), p. 18 (emphasis in the original); cf. also 'Les Conseils ouvriers' in the same issue. *Front noir*, a journal with surrealist origins, shares this attitude: 'The workers will only act for the revolution by becoming conscious of the human values of socialism.' The motivation for this acceptance of consciousness can only be ethical; *Front noir*, 4–5 (May 1964), p. 12.

32. *Cahiers de discussion pour le socialisme de conseils*, 7 (November 1966), 'Notes sur le progrès de la richesse et de la misère'. *Front noir*, which starts from the same assumptions, does not reach the same conclusions as the *Cahiers* with regard to organization: 'SR' asserts that a revolutionary organization can, without exercising any 'authoritarian function', play a part in the creation and development of revolutionary consciousness; see Nos. 4–5, quoted above.

acquire an awareness of the inhuman nature of bourgeoi
institutions?' A study also needs to be made of the views of a
group which has resolved this problem of the 'birth of revo
lutionary consciousness' in a different manner and has pushe
the spontaneist thesis to the limits of its potential.

The group 'Informations correspondance ouvrières' (ICO
is the result of a split in Socialisme ou Barbarie. The 'minority
faction were opposed both to the highly 'Leninist' organiza
tional theories of the majority group and to the interna
organization of the group, which they maintained ought to b
more flexible. In October 1958, the split became final and th
minority faction formed the 'Informations liaison ouvrières
group, which changed its name in June 1960 to 'Information
correspondance ouvrières'. Originally there were two paralle
formations – a discussion group and an 'inter-factory' group
After 1962, only the latter survived, since the tasks of liaiso
and information seemed more important to some activists tha
attempts at theorizing.

The rejection of all 'prophetic' thinking stemmed from a ver
literal interpretation of the slogan, 'the emancipation of th
workers must come from the workers themselves', and from a
particular attitude to the class struggle. To the ICO group, th
class struggle will inevitably result in the running of factorie
and of society by the workers. It is therefore up to the workers
and to them alone, to defend their interests and fight for thei
own emancipation.[33] Their deeds and their exploits, thei
victories and their defeats, are the very stuff of the clas
struggle. This may be seen as the *saga* of the working class
which outside interference will only distract from its objective
In the past, the working class fought for a number of claim
intended to satisfy the economic needs of the workers an
ensure them a minimum of well-being and security. It was the
a question of a 'life or death' struggle leading to social vic
tories which have now become institutionalized. The trans
formations of the modern world, the increase in knowledg

33. cf. the declaration of intent reproduced on the back of the journa
Informations et correspondance ouvrières : 'Ce que nous sommes, ce qu
nous voulons' ('What we are, what we want').

and welfare have rendered most of the conceptions we have inherited from the past obsolete. The behaviour of the workers is now governed by new conceptions, it is the result of transformations in modern capitalism, of fundamental divisions between directors and operatives, of the alienation of consumption.[34] Today, the struggle has taken new forms and is directed towards new objectives. The new opposition questions the whole principle of working for a wage, all hierarchies, all authority. Thus to the militants of the ICO it is the process of struggle which brings about an evolution in the mentality of the working class, itself linked to the structures of capitalist enterprises. The behaviour of the workers is in a sense 'stimulated' by the socio-economic environment, to which it responds by a series of confrontations (wildcat strikes, across-the-board claims by-passing the hierarchy) which in turn provoke further reactions and new developments.[35] This 'dialectical' progress of the workers' struggle combines, in their experience of production, both actual social structures and their own *consciousness*, which develops in step with the changes that occur within capitalist society. They are therefore obliged to struggle against the parties, trade unions and splinter groups which litter their path. They in fact pursue the fight alone, and they pursue it on the shop floor. Social and cultural structures will result from the suppression of the exploitative system, and the alienations that weigh on the worker in his everyday life cannot be singled out for separate attack.[36]

This view of the class struggle leads on to a critique of working-class organizations which is a logical extension of it. The parties, it is claimed, operate according to criteria and towards objectives that are foreign to the class struggle. As for

34. Simon: 'Travailleurs, syndicats et militants', *Noir et Rouge*, 19 November 1961). This gives a fairly full summary of the ICO position, defining at the same time the group's 'line'; *Informations et correspondance ouvrières*, 29 (May 1964), p. 13.

35. 'Organisation et mouvement ouvrier', in *Informations et correspondance ouvrières*, 79 (March 1969).

36. cf. the discussion with the Noir et Rouge group in the report of activities reproduced in *Informations et liaison ouvrières*, 41 (17 September 1959).

the trade unions, they are organs of administration and not of struggle. They are 'dispensers of advantages' and are treated as such by the workers. They cannot be said to have 'degenerated', since they never fulfilled any function other than that of social conservation. To the ICO, the main thing is that the workers should be aware of the real nature of the unions, and not take them to be something they are not. From this assertion, the reasoning is extended to all working-class organizations that hope to 'play a part' in the struggle. This ambition appears absurd, for the conceptions of the workers cannot be formed arbitrarily by trade-union, party or other propaganda. They are the 'natural' product of the present form of the class struggle, on the basis of which the workers will project the future form of their organizations of struggle.[37] In these circumstances, there is no room for a permanent revolutionary organization. Such organizations inevitably adapt to the ambient state of capitalist society. The struggle is pursued day by day in a multitude of forms; in the last analysis, it fuses with the everyday life of the worker on the shop floor. The formation of autonomous fighting committees would indicate that the revolution had already started. To agitate for the creation of such committees would amount to advising the workers to start a revolution ...[38]

The spontaneist ideas of the ICO would seem to lead to an 'organizational void', and they have been reproached with encouraging 'non-organization and disenchantment'.[39] However, militancy is not excluded in itself, and the very existence of the group bears witness to this. It is designed on an individual basis to help the workers 'to do what they want' and to prevent anything being organized at factory level without their agreement. The militant is therefore supposed to act towards workers' self-determination. Any other form of militancy would result in pure activism, identical with that of traditional organ-

37. *Informations et correspondance ouvrières*, 36 (February 1965), p. 15.
38. 'Travailleurs, syndicats et militants', art. cit.
39. cf., for instance, the article by a member of the ICO entitled 'La Différence', *Informations et correspondance ouvrières*, 81 (May 1969), pp. 18–19.

izations. To hope to 'play a part' entails becoming an agent of change in present society, but not of its liberation, whatever the 'subjective' intention governing such a project.[40] In other words, militancy should not consist in sharing certain ideas held to be 'true' or 'good' but in acting in such a manner as to help the workers to 'understand where their interests as workers lie'. The militant must pursue the struggle as a worker, not as a member of an organization, even a shop-floor organization. Shop-floor organizations can only exist within limited periods of struggle, and must be set up by the workers themselves, from the inside.[41] Outside the factory, the only form of organization conceivable is horizontal coordination designed to facilitate links between isolated workers and publish 'shop' information. Within such a group (incarnated, for example, by the ICO) the participants provide information on what is going on in their respective places of work, 'condemn the manipulations of the trade unions', discuss their common claims and provide mutual aid.[42]

The class struggle as conceived by ICO should result in workers' control of society. Is it possible to foresee its precise forms? Certainly the ICO is attached to the historical councilist movement, to the extent indeed that it publishes historical texts, discusses them and endeavours to re-enact them.[43] It has also happened that some of its members have supported the notion that the proletarian struggle must of necessity result in a specially privileged form of council, the purest expression of that struggle.[44] But it would seem that the group as a whole,

40. ibid., No. 80 (April 1969), 'Organisation et mouvement ouvrier', p. 15. Cf. also the issue published as a supplement to No. 55 (December 1966), entitled: 'Qu'est-ce que l'organisation?'

41. *Informations et correspondance ouvrières*, 36 (February 1965), p. 18.

42. 'Ce que nous sommes, ce que nous voulons', quoted earlier.

43. cf., for example, the issue devoted to the 'Mouvement pour les conseils ouvriers en Allemagne' ('Workers' Councils Movement in Germany'), 42 (August–September 1965), which also contains a discussion of this subject. Reprinted in No. 101 (February 1971).

44. cf., for example, in No. 42, quoted above, p. 4 of the Appendix: 'Correspondance-Discussion'.

refusing to 'anticipate the society of the future', is reluctant to pronounce upon the forms which the revolution and future society are to take, and hence to make propaganda in favour of council communism. This is the main feature distinguishing it from another group, otherwise very close to it, which considers the historical forms of the council movement to be the ones that must be adopted in the coming revolution. Whereas to the ICO the council movement was one of the forms of autonomous struggle historically adopted by the labour movement, the 'Communisme de conseils' group is by contrast attached to the councillist movement on the grounds that it is in itself the incarnation of communism. It therefore aims at 'relating' theory to practice by analysing recent events in the light of councillist theory as handed down by O. Rühle, H. Gorter, A. Pannekoek and others. Council communism would thus be more than a history lesson – it would be *the* theory, which needs both to be propagated and enriched.[45]

The theory of council communism, therefore, is far from homogeneous. We have examined the principle notions which subtend it, from the ideas of *Socialisme ou Barbarie* which, at one extreme, lie at the boundary between councils and party, to those of the ICO which has managed to dissolve the theory itself into the spontaneity of struggle and the conceptions which arise from it. The very source of council communism (a segment of Marxism, variously interpreted) has exercised different influences on the heirs of the historic movement. Some dissociate themselves from the tradition, others less so. Some accept and adopt the critique of everyday life, others, like ICO, regard it as secondary to the critique of the system of economic exploitation. But all the trends mentioned unite in condemnation of the Marxist–Leninist movement. In addition, all have certain ideas regarding the degree of autonomy necessary to the working-class struggle, and its spontaneity. Although with varying degrees of emphasis, they have also extended their

45. cf. the *Cahiers du communisme de conseils*, No. 1 (October 1968), 'Notre tâche'; No. 5 (March 1970), 'Éditorial' and 'Bolchevisme et communisme de conseils'; and No. 6 (June 1970), 'L'auto-mouvement des travailleurs').

ideas into the field of organization, both of the revolutionary movement and of the future socialist society.

Above all, however, all these trends, whether surrealist in origin or Marxist (Trotskyist or ultra-left), acknowledge and identify with the *contestation* movement of the last five years. And all new theoretical work has revolved around the contest being fought out in modern society.

5. *Leftism and active dissent*

To leftism, the relationships between leftist theory and revolutionary practice are obvious. The former tries to express the latter, sometimes to herald it, less often to inspire it. We have already seen the position which leftist theory assigns itself in the evolution of the radical movement. It hardly aspires to more than being the concept behind an unformulated reality. This is the reverse of the Kautskyist–Leninist conception which borrows so heavily from the infatuation with science that characterized the closing years of the nineteenth century. Historical reality was deduced from historical *laws*, and Marxism represented the *law* of socio-economic movement. The theoreticians were at once in possession of the abstract knowledge of this law and, as leaders of the labour movement, they had a monopoly of its historical interpretation. The proletarian was only supposed to acquire knowledge of its own practice in the field of economics; its spontaneity ceased at the threshold of science. The real movement, in order to break into the territory of politics, must be organized by professional revolutionaries, to accomplish tasks of which only theory could give cognizance. To borrow the language of philosophy, the working class could only become a *class in itself* when properly led.

Leftism has effected a complete reversal of perspective: revolutionary consciousness *is* the product of struggle. The workers are both actors in the drama of history and its producers. Any intrusion from outside alters the very circumstances of the struggle and distorts its progress. Consequently the sway held by ideologies of Marxist origin over the labour movement have not necessarily enriched the class struggle; the 'revolutionary battles' so vaunted by Stalinist mythology were for the most part defeats, beginning with the October Revolution. All outside intervention changes the course of working-class praxis, much as the introduction of a foreign body may completely modify a chemical reaction. There are, of course, gradations in the conceptions of spontaneity which may, in extreme cases, dissolve in tautology. But it remains a principle that a theory may be the expression of a real movement, may even divine it by anticipation, but may *not* lead it, as do those ideologies which, far from enlightening the proletarian consciousness, mystify it and divert the struggle from its proper course.

The question which now arises is that of the link between the theory and the practice of the revolutionary movement. Even without being 'imposed', an intellectual system may very well influence behaviour, inflect it, even guide it. There are many intermediate stages between information pure and simple and ideology, many levels through which the consciousness may pass, from purely 'objective' influence to 'brain-washing'.

The second question that arises is that of the *congruence* of theory and practice. It is certain that a theory which finds no verification in the varied tapestry of social events would be pure utopia.[1] The reason why so many sociologists take the trouble to make a study of leftism is because they occasionally see in it something more than material for a chapter on the history of ideas. But to what extent does leftism partake of social theory rather than philosophy?

In order to answer the first question, one is led, obviously, to speak of the practice of social conflict. There has been much talk of the powerful influence of Marcuse, Rudi Dutschke and Henri Lefebvre. But what *praxis* are we talking about? That of university lecturers, students, agricultural workers, white-collar workers, craftsmen? Far from denying the enormous influence which the expression of opinions and the spread of ideas may have on social behaviour,[2] I think it quite impossible to assess,

1. Which does not mean to say that utopia has no hold at all over the real, and indeed leftism frequently claims to favour the introduction of an element of utopianism into real life. But that is a problem beyond the terms of reference of this chapter.

2. Opinion polls, to mention but one source, have sufficiently demonstrated the decisive effect that a speech or particular doctrine may have on behaviour (electoral behaviour, for example). This influence is not necessarily positive, for before the seed can germinate it must fall upon fertile soil.

at the present time, the importance of the part played by radical ideas transmitted from outside in unleashing and promoting the current practice of active dissent. It varies, moreover, as between strikers and students, and almost nothing is known of the motives of the strikers in the occupied factories. Even less is known of the *development* (or lack of it) in these motives. For despite all the valuable studies that have been carried out in the way of surveys and journalistic reports, hardly any questionnaire has been drawn up that makes mention of the influence of such and such a doctrine or such and such a slogan. Even so, the influence of certain ideas would have to be *conscious*, which is by no means always the case. In short, social psychology and sociology have up to now played no part in the study of the practice of active dissent.[3] At the same time, it seems to me preferable to avoid making forays into divination or applying methods derived from 'intuitive reasoning'.

However, certain hypotheses – and even some certainties – do spring to mind that have been freely aired. After 10–11 May 1968, the 'Student Commune' was adopted by the people. Independent broadcasting stations provided unexpected propaganda by publicizing not only the exploits of the dissenting students but their ideas as well. It has been asserted that the occupation of factories after the 14 May 'was in imitation of the occupation of the Sorbonne'; that the slogans circulating in the Latin Quarter were immediately taken up by the strikers or future strikers. That is possible. It should not be forgotten, however, that wildcat strikes and factory occupations accompanied by violent confrontations with the police had already taken place in 1966, 1967 and the beginning of 1968. In Caen, for example, on 26 January 1968, it was the students who joined the strikers of SAVIEM demonstrating in the town. At Rhodiaceta in Bescançon in February–March 1967, it was again the strikers who organized a permanent fair on the site of the occupied factory, invited troupes of actors to give theatrical performances and invited the local population (students among them) to join with them. In order to be cer-

3. With regard to the factual studies which have been made, the reader is directed to Denis Woronoff: 'Pour une histoire de mai', *Politique aujourd'hui* (August-September 1969), which gives a selected list.

tain of the 'exemplary' nature of the Latin Quarter revolt, it would be necessary to conduct many more interviews and inquiries. The fact remains that there was 'communication' between two worlds which up to that time had remained closed to each other; first through the medium of broadcasting, then by direct contact. From the night of the 10–11 May, young workers joined the barricades . . .[4] After 13 May, 'adults' from every kind of background and all social classes converged on the Sorbonne. Subsequently, 'joint' worker–student action committees were created. Under cover of these committees, numerous students were able to enter the factories, especially in the early days and even the early hours of the strike. Discussions were held between strikers and students.[5] Finally, mention should be made of the innumerable wall posters, pamphlets and journals which were not intended only for the students' benefit. Above all, hundreds of thousands of tracts were distributed in the streets and in the factories (although here the students frequently met with lively resistance from the strike committees).

It can be concluded with certainty that numerous contacts were established between students and workers (especially during May–June 1968). It may even be postulated that leftist ideas were not entirely without influence in the progressive 'politicization' of many strikers and on the current forms of social conflict. But beyond these cautious hypotheses, we enter the realm of conjecture. Especially if we hope to specify the *extent* to which social dissent was influenced and inspired by modern leftist theory. The share attributable to leftist ideas and the hold they have acquired on the practice of active dissent remain indeterminate.[6]

If we now consider a longer period, extending from 1963–5

4. P. Vidal-Naquet reports their presence. A. Schnapp, P. Vidal-Naquet, *Journal de la Commune étudiante* (Paris, 1969), p. 41.

5. Some records of these exist (notably on film), cf., for example, for Nantes; *Les Cahiers de mai*, 1 (15 June 1968).

6. I have refrained from mentioning a factor which might increase this uncertainty: the diversity of leftist ideas and the multiplicity of their sources. Extremist propaganda frequently took over 'spontaneist' ideas, while at the same time amalgamating them with 'directives' that were Trotskyist or Maoist in origin.

to 1971, it may be asked whether leftist themes did not become mingled with ideologies of working-class origin, such as revolutionary syndicalism and anarcho-syndicalism. It has been seen that leftism adopted, among others, themes that were part of a working-class tradition going back to the revolutionary period from 1789–94. Leftism has carried with it a whole fund of images and attitudes that are deeply rooted in the revolutionary traditions.[7] The marches, songs and barricades have been compared with the sequence of events during the Paris Commune.[8] Some have gone further still, in identifying the collective representations and the claims of the leftists with the 'dream' of total emancipation entertained by revolutionary syndicalism.[9]

All such historical recollections are undoubtedly interesting, but it would be more fruitful to establish the thread via which the historical tradition has been transmitted. The case of revolutionary syndicalism is an interesting one, since in its direct action, its anti-parliamentarianism, its anti-interventionism and its anti-Marxism it contains a number of elements of modern leftism. There are two objections to it, however, the first relating to the 'guardians' of the anarcho-syndicalist tradition, and the second to the *syndical* nature of that tradition. Let us consider the two in turn.

It would seem difficult to maintain that the tradition of revolutionary syndicalism has been transmitted to the mass of the workers by the two organizations who are its avowed exponents. The first is the group of revolutionary syndicalists

7. For example, the revived practice of holding general meetings (of workshops, of whole factories) under conditions of direct democracy irresistibly remind one of the life of the *sections* during the French Revolution, reconstructed with great erudition by A. Souboul in his *Les Sans-culottes* (Paris, 1968).

8. cf. M. Rebérioux, 'Tout ça n'empêche pas, Nicolas, que la Commune n'est pas morte' ('For all that, Nicholas, the Commune is not dead'), *Politique aujourd'hui*, 5 (May 1969), and P. Vidal-Naquet, *Journal de la Commune étudiante*, Introduction.

9. G. Adam, 'Mai ou les leçons de l'histoire ouvrière' ('May, or the Lessons of Working-Class History') in *France Forum*, 90–91 (October–November 1968).

centred on the journal *La Révolution prolétarienne* (founded in 1925 by P. Monatte), which seems to have virtually no influence in the factories. The journal itself seems principally occupied in 'keeping the flame burning' rather than engaging in practical proselytism. The same observation applies to the National Confederation of Labour (CNT, the French branch of the International Working-men's Association), a tiny trade union composed principally of anarcho-syndicalist workers and whose newspaper, *Combat syndicaliste* (which has at certain periods in its history been published in Spanish), keeps alive the memory of the Spanish CNT and more generally of the anarcho-syndicalist tradition, but whose readership rarely rises above 2,000 to 3,000.

Paradoxically, the standard-bearer of the revolutionary syndicalist tradition in modern times is, according to some hypotheses, the contemporary CFDT, whose origins are closer to social Catholicism than to the Charter of Amiens. At the same time, the second objection, that relating to the *syndical* or trade-union nature of this tradition, is an even more serious one, and will be dealt with after considering the above hypothesis.

The CFTC had originally been a working-class organization closer to the Catholic hierarchy than to the trade-union tradition. The 1939–44 war saw a change in the Confederation, from the very fact of the anti-Pétainist, pro-Resistance attitude of many CFTC militants and leaders. After 1946, the Confederation returned to the tradition of trade-union independence, and from that moment the left-wing minority attempted to hold to an authentically working-class line in opposition to the communism of the CGT majority. Organized in groups calling themselves Reconstruction, this left wing adopted the traditional syndicalist line, and ensured that the trade-union federation developed, after the 1952 Congress, towards a programme of democratic socialism conceived primarily in economic terms, and owing more to the revolutionary syndicalism of the pre-1914 era than to Marxism.[10] After the 1964 Congress, the

10. cf. P. Vignaux: 'Evolution et problèmes de la CFTC' in *La Nef*, 5 (January 1954); and S. H. Barnes: 'The Politics of French Christian Labor', *The Journal of Politics*, XXI, No. 1 (February 1959).

congress which broke the direct links with the Church and resulted in schism (a vestigial 'Loyalist CFTC' still survives), the Confederation became more political and swung to the left, a development made possible by the accession, in 1961, of the old minority to the leading positions in the union.

The Reconstruction minority had long been the trustees of the old-style pre-1914 syndicalism. In opposition to the CGT, linked to the Communist Party, and the FO, which claimed to be apolitical, it demanded that the CFTC continue the French tradition of revolutionary syndicalism, 're-thought' in the light of new circumstances.[11] The Reconstruction groups hoped to distil, out of the history of the French labour movement, a form of socialism that was both democratic and had an economic viewpoint. This attitude led the CFDT, after 1964, to present itself as the sole heir of the pre-1914 CGT and to adopt a number of the latter's slogans and watchwords: it refused to ally itself to a party, it aspired to lead an economic revolution, it believed in doctrinal diversity and in direct action.

After May–June 1968, the Confederation again confirmed this development by its attitude to the general strike and by the stance it adopted subsequently. The Thirty-fifth Congress of the CFDT (held in May 1970) consecrated the new radical stand taken by the Federation's Bureau by recognizing the class struggle and placing workers' control among its list of objectives. Between 1967 and 1970 the Confederation gave the impression of having moved from representing an opposition from within the system to active dissent and *contestation* from outside it.[12] To some of the *cédétiste* leaders, workers' control provides the solution to the problem of authority: in a socialism run on cooperative lines, it would emanate from the base, so

11. This theme has been illustrated and extended by R. Mouriaux and J. Capdevielle in their contribution to a seminar held in the third session of the National Foundation of Political Sciences, a duplicated document of twelve pages entitled: 'Transmission et déplacement du syndicalisme révolutionnaire'.

12. On the Thirty-fifth Congress, see J. Julliard, 'La CFDT au pied du mur', *Esprit* (July–August 1970). The standpoint taken by the union in the month of May 1968 is detailed in the special issue of *Syndicalisme* of November 1969 (No. 1266 A).

realizing true direct democracy, which is absent from régimes where the economy is state-controlled or mixed. Others see direct action and workers' control as the best means of 'smashing the authoritarian model of the ruling class'.[13] In short, the recent positions adopted by the CFDT leadership are directed towards making it a common meeting-point for all the workers radicalized in the struggles of recent years.

There is no doubt that this leftward movement of the union is not entirely unequivocal. There have been many ready to point out that the infrequent renewal of the leading caucus, the wide political spectrum (from the traditional right to the 'leftists' of Hacuitex) found at every level of the leadership, the imprint of social Catholicism in the attitudes of many long-standing members and militants mean that the development towards the 'class struggle' position adopted by the Thirty-fifth Congress is not always entirely credible.[14] This makes recent statements by the CFDT somewhat suspect, which brings us back to the leftist objection that the watchwords it has put out over the past few years such as 'planning', 'participation', 'structural reform' are difficult to reconcile with a cooperatively based socialist society under workers' control. Finally, it is the very fact that it is a trade union which places it, in the eyes of the thinking leftist groups, in the ranks of those organizations working for 'social conservation'.

So, despite all its efforts, the CFDT finds itself branded with the original sin of being a trade union. Consequently the ideology of the CFDT finds no place within the framework of the leftist theories considered in this work, which are typified by a virulent anti-trade-unionism. However, in examining possible 'points of contact' between leftist theory and the practice of active dissent, one should not overlook the fact that the CFDT *might* have provided an organizational framework for leftist activity. Since well before 1968 it appeared, by

13. A. Détraz and E. Maire, 'Pourquoi nous croyons à l'autogestion', in *Preuves* (fourth quarter, 1970). Cf. also *La CFDT* (Paris, 1971), Part 2.

14. This ambiguity has been underlined by P. Capdevielle in 'La CFDT depuis 1968', *Projet* (November 1970).

comparison with the CGT and the FO, a 'dynamic' union, allowing 'hard-line' initiatives decided upon by the rank and file,[15] so that, rightly or wrongly, it acquired a reputation as a democratic union. The part played by the CFDT in May–June 1968, the sympathy it expressed for the 'Student Commune', the stand it took in favour of grass-roots democracy and of the need for free and open discussion attracted a number of young dissenters who felt themselves to be close to leftism. It is therefore not impossible that the CFDT, through its declared readiness to allow the workers to assume the responsibility for formulating claims and preparing and carrying out industrial action themselves,[16] may have served as a broadcasting centre for some leftist ideas on direct action, mistrust of State authority, and the importance of action stemming from the rank and file. However, it is still not possible to be certain about the extent to which the CFDT initiated action or merely acted as a catalyst, or to which the workers joining it were *already* imbued with a considerable dose of combativeness rather than acquiring it through contact with the union.

On the other hand, more information is available on the influence which leftist ideas exercised on student dissent. The question here is not to determine the precise degree of such influence, but merely to note, with the aid of some indicators, the *points of contact*.

Leftist theory found a highly effective soil in student circles.[17] From the mid-sixties onwards, small groups existed which proclaimed their allegiance to this or that aspect of leftism. Most important of all, however, most of the 'radical' journals circu-

15. In the months preceding the general strike of 1968, most of the 'wildcat' action had taken place in factories where the CFDT was in a majority over the CGT; cf. my article 'The Ideology and Practice of Contestation seen through Recent Events in France', *Government and Opposition*, V, No. 4 (Autumn 1970).

16. *La CFDT*, p. 178 (declaration by André Jeanson). It should also be remembered that the 'radicalization' of the CFDT corresponded to a 'sobering-up' of the CGT which, at its 1969 congress, modified Article 2 of its Statutes relating to the abolition of the wage system.

17. Although, paradoxically, it was not intended for students but for the workers, the revolutionary class *par excellence*.

lated in the universities: *Socialisme ou Barbarie, Noir et Rouge, Pouvoir ouvrier, Internationale situationniste*, etc.[18] The latter even possessed more or less avowed disciples who carried out 'exemplary' agitation under various labels ('Enragés', 'Vandales') in a number of university towns (Paris, Nanterre, Strasbourg, Bordeaux, Nantes). Tracts originating from the situationists or the neo-anarchists were already questioning the bourgeois structure of the university, the transmission of a fixed, static culture, the bureaucracy and authoritarianism of the system. The situationists had aimed at drafting a 'practical theory' which would make it possible both to analyse the alienations of the modern world and to fight that world in everyday life. The Strasbourg 'scandal' served both as a general statement and as a model of this aim. Not only had the cyberneticist Abraham Moles been prevented from giving his classes, but the UNEF branch and the local BAPU (Bureau of University Psychiatric Aid) had been dissolved. From the academic year 1966–7, an extremely energetic movement of student agitation was created, which claimed to reject the human sciences as an instrument of repression and manipulation of the masses. The themes underlying the motives for these acts of dissent might have been approved by Marcuse or Reich. And yet leftist theory did not explicitly take up the heritage of Freudo-Marxism. Both Marcuse and W. Reich were known to a minority of leftist theoreticians, but to the majority they were probably not even names.[19] On the other hand, the essentials of leftist preoccupations (*contestation* of the leadership principle, of the principle of authority, de-alienation of everyday life) harmonized perfectly with Freudo-Marxism. Psychology and sociology students have been very receptive to Marcusian themes relating to the adaptation function of (neo-Freudian) psychoanalysis

18. This is also confirmed by P. Vidal-Naquet, *Journal de la Commune étudiante*, Introduction.

19. A. Frankin wrote a highly lucid article on W. Reich and the sexual economy in *Arguments*, 18 (second quarter, 1960). The same issue reproduced a lecture read by Marcuse to the Ecole des Hautes Etudes in 1958–9 ('De l'ontologie à la technologie'). Chaulieu, for his part, was 'contaminated' by the ideas of Marcuse from 1961–2, but never gave a systematic account of them.

and its political possibilities in the search for a non-repressive society. In 1966 the publishers F. Maspero brought out a special edition of the review *Partisans* (Nos. 32–3, October–December 1966) devoted to the subject of 'Sexuality and Repression', and at the beginning of 1967 the sexologist Boris Fraenkel gave a lecture on W. Reich to the students at Nanterre. In January 1967 a sexology exhibition was organized, in the course of which a number of papers were circulated. Debates were also held in which proposals to 'update' Freudo-Marxism were made. In the foreword to a duplicated pamphlet distributed during the exhibition, which contained the transcript of a lecture read by H. Marcuse to the students of the Sorbonne in 1962 and an article by the psychoanalyst I. Caruso, the problem of sexual liberation was put very clearly.[20] 'Far from believing', the authors of the preface write, 'that sexual liberation is a precondition of the social revolution, we consider that the precise opposite is true. Enlarging the struggle of the proletariat and making it into not only a global, economic and political struggle, but also a cultural and moral one is no way to resolve it.' They conclude that it is necessary to 'mobilize all forces ... necessary to the destruction of the existing social system, and effect a revision of the social order in terms of earthly happiness'. Finally, in March 1968, extracts of a manifesto published by Reich in 1936 were distributed on the occasion of a conference organized at Nanterre by the Resident Students' Association of the University of Nanterre on the theme of 'Sexuality and Repression'. This paper, which had in fact been in circulation for more than a year, made a frontal attack on sexual morality, the family structure and marriage in its present form, and issued a denunciation of 'sexual chaos'.[21]

20. Twenty-page roneoed brochure entitled 'Eléments pour une critique révolutionnaire de la répression sexuelle' ('Elements of a Revolutionary Critique of Sexual Repression'). Marcuse's text is titled 'Répression sociale et répression psychologique, actualité politique de Freud' ('Social and Psychological Repression : the Political Modernity of Freud'), and that of Caruso, 'L'ambivalence dans la société du bien-être' ('Ambivalence in the Affluent Society'). Both articles are accompanied by commentaries and a selective bibliography on the problems dealt with.

21. Extracts reproduced in the *Journal de la Commune étudiante*, pp.

There can be no doubt that the critique of everyday life found a very potent propaganda medium in this: sexual problems and problems relating to the 'cut-and-dried' nature of education, to the 'scientific neutrality' of disciplines such as sociology, psychology and psychoanalysis were the very ones that formed the chief preoccupations of the average student. This explains why the disturbances at Nanterre began with a question put publicly by a student to a minister (who had come to officiate at the opening of the campus swimming-pool) on the subject of the 'sexual indigence' of the young, and why the first serious confrontations with the administration took place on the subject of the university rule prohibiting visits to the women's quarters. Finally, it explains the constant interruptions of lessons in objection to the 'neutrality' of the social sciences. The question, 'Why do we need sociologists'?, was rapidly transformed into, 'Why do we need the University?', into a debate on the university's role. Boycotting of examinations and lessons and the movement for self-government within the university resounded like a distant echo of Marcuse's ideas on the part played by universities as agents of social integration, even of manipulation.

After May–June 1968, Freudo-Marxism became widely and rapidly propagated. By now Reich, even more than Marcuse, has joined the pantheon of the precursors of leftism. He owes this in particular to his ideas on the social roots of neurosis, on the social function of sexual repression and on the role played by the patriarchal family in the perpetuation of the repressive society. This is a point of contact between the theory and practice of dissent which seems to me to be of extreme importance in the long term, especially so far as dissent among school-children and young workers is concerned.

If we now consider the question of *contestation* itself, in its widest sense (in factories, offices, secondary schools, universities), independent of all possible influences on the part of

---

132–3. The same text was also published in its entirety in the Sorbonne during the students' sit-in, in the form of enormous hand-written mural posters. It seems likely that it was by this means that most of the students first became aware of Reich's teaching.

theoretical leftism, independent of the areas where theory and practice may have met and provided one another with reciprocal nourishment (and therefore leaving aside the sociologically important question of *points of contact*), a number of observations may be made.

First of all leftist theory, in contrast to 'orthodox' Marxism, does not pretend to be a scientific theory of social development. Consequently, it does not trouble to scrutinize history (whether past or contemporary) in order to deduce the correct praxis. This simple observation has very significant consequences, as has been seen, on the question of revolutionary consciousness and, by extension, on that of organization. But it also suggests why the question of the relation between leftist theory and practice is not put in terms of the *influence* the former may have on the latter. Not that this type of consideration is negligible, particularly for the historian or the sociologist of the labour movement, but it is a *theoretically* inessential question. For leftist theory claims to *express* the real, not to formulate it, even less to model it. It claims to be the concept of a concrete movement, and does not hesitate to *anticipate* the latter, for the movement of history is not irrational. But nothing guarantees that the class struggle will take the form which is *theoretically* accorded to it. Projections are therefore a matter of probabilities, not certainties. These only exist in the praxis of the movement.

The important factor, then, is the concrete form which the real movement will assume. If it confirms that which claims to be its own concept, then in truth the theory is a true revolutionary theory. If, on the other hand, it invalidates it, the theory is downgraded to the level of an *ideology* or utopia (which may itself be a form of false consciousness).

It may indeed appear paradoxical that the question of the practice, and hence of the well-foundedness of the theory is posed at the very end of a volume entirely devoted to abstract conceptions. Should this question not have been put at the beginning, that is to say the question of whether the practice of *contestation* has confirmed the supposed rationalization made of it? This would have been logical, but impracticable. The leftists observe that the practice of independent struggle has been stifled and rendered almost impossible over the past half-century. Conceptual reflection has therefore had to be based on indications, on fragmentary conflicts that have broken through the veneer of Stalinist totalitarianism, both in the Soviet Union and, so far as the labour movement is concerned, in the West. But even though it is possible that the autonomous pursuit of struggle has been retarded by the tight grip maintained by the CPSU on the proletariat of a large number of industrialized countries, the low economic and spiritual level of the proletariat would certainly have inhibited the full expression of this aim.

On the contrary, and this links up with the latter observation, the new turn taken by the class struggle in recent years has confirmed the predictions of the most lucid of the councillists, the Dutch, who in the years before the last war staunchly maintained, in the face of general opposition, that the struggle would take the form of increasingly violent wildcat strikes.

This is the point of view held by the theoretical leftists; what does the reality look like? If we consider the period from 1967 to 1971, and consider France in isolation, changes took place in the mode of social conflict that few observers will deny. To some sociologists, 1968 even inaugurated a new period of social struggle, while others saw it as a new life-style that had been introduced. A whole new historical epoch was commencing.[22] This judgement is regarded as optimistic by others, who see in the strike of May 1968 nothing more than a strike. The important thing, clearly, is to catalogue the social conflicts which took place in order to determine whether anything really new emerges and, even more important, whether this new feature has any chance of permanence.

An initial balance-sheet of the practice of social conflict must take account of two factors: firstly, the small number of

22. For different interpretations of the social *contestation* of May–June 1968, cf. P. Bénéton and J. Touchard, 'Les Interprétations de la crise de mai–juin 1968', *Revue française de science politique*, XX, 3 (June 1970), notably pp. 523 and 529; and P. Souyri, 'La crise de mai', *Annales*, 1 (January–February 1970), notably pp. 179 and 184.

sociological surveys that have so far been carried out, and secondly the brief duration of the period under consideration (five years at most).[23] Given these reservations, one cannot fail to be struck by the spread of a number of practices that have broken new ground. Not because such and such a practice was previously unknown (for example recourse to a general ballot of the work-force at a works meeting to decide on whether to strike or call a strike off, or even on a wildcat strike), but that their combined presence makes it possible to speak of a new *mode* of social conflict. The whole range of these practices (considered over the period from 1967 to 1970) is characterized by the following features: strikes break out outside the framework of the union machine, and often against the union's advice (where it is even consulted), and are often accompanied by occupation of the premises (offices, factory grounds, pits). The strike is called by the whole work-force and for an *unlimited* period. Claims are not categorized (e.g. an equal wage increase for the whole work-force), and in addition to financial advantages they are directed towards achieving 'qualitative' improvements: in the hierarchical structure of the company, in the wage system as such (in particular the practice of incentive payments and bonus schemes), in the management of the factory and a whole series of changes relating to the life of the worker in his employment (lateness, clocking-in, conditions of work). The progress of a strike will follow a particular pattern: the strike committee will include both organized *and non-union* workers, and all the workers affected will pronounce upon all questions relating to the strike at the general works meeting, and in particular will appoint or dismiss the members of the strike committee and of the delegation that negotiates with the employer. There may be 'sorties' from the works: demonstrations in the streets, marches to the Préfecture (or other public building), confrontations with the police.

Finally, it may be observed that this type of strike has tended

23. I have attempted, with the aid of existing material, to draw an outline of the current modes of (industrial) conflict in 'The Ideology and Practice of Contestation', *Government and Opposition*, V, 4 (Autumn 1970).

to take place in the bigger plants, characterized by greater social mobility, by a high percentage of young workers (often under 21 years of age) and in which the CFDT is more strongly represented than the CGT.

Of course this description is of an 'ideal type' of *contestation* strike, based on a certain number of concrete instances. By and large, this is still an atypical phenomenon, which only occurs in some strikes in some sectors. Most of these features were more vividly apparent in May–June 1968, but they still survive today. It should be noted that in many cases the 'autonomous' structure born of the strike (shop-floor strike committee, general works committee) persists for some time after the end of the dispute. To obtain a more complete picture of the practice of *contestation*, mention should be made of the conflicts which have occurred in the schools, universities, prisons and among consumers (Métro passengers, council tenants, users of crèches and play groups, etc.).

The limitations of this account are, however, apparent: the number of examples studied have been small (except for May–June 1968), the surveys conducted originated from different sources applying different methods, the period of study has been too short to be truly significant, or to enable one to speak of a structural rather than a merely conjunctural tendency. It would be especially important to determine whether this type of conflict represents the majority of cases, whether they affect key sectors and whether they are likely to become the rule.

This said, the characteristics enumerated above all bear witness to a high degree of spontaneity, to what the leftists call 'autonomy of struggle'. It is true that the influence of the trade-union machine (or for that matter the party machine or the political cell) is minimal at the beginning of a strike (since the CFDT allows greater freedom of initiative to the rank and file), and that the types of claim bear witness to the opposition that exists to certain structures (the wage structure, the structure of authority, hierarchies, trade unionism) and to a desire, often unexpressed, to take over the management of the company. In this sense, the practice of *contestation* does correspond to the analyses made by leftist theory. The leftists have not been slow to identify with the current trend towards *contestation*. To them, the extension and development of the struggle (and its reproduction in other countries would give further confirmation of their ideas giving them *universal* validity) brings the modern world and the real movement into a historical phase of which leftism provides the most complete theoretical expression.

Epilogue

Leftism as I have tried to present it is far from being a finished, coherent theory. It is rather a collection of elements of critique, analysis and constructive conceptions. However, this confers sufficient coherence to make it legitimate to bring these elements together into a single conceptual framework. For leftism represents a common inspiration, a common vision of the world and projection of the future. The heterogeneity of its constituents, their occasional apparent incompatibility, also arises from the fact that this theory is not yet fully realized. It has been held up to examination at a moment when the fusion is not complete; at the present time, anything can still happen: the various contributory currents may separate, they may become individualized outside the main stream, or they may become fused in the same crucible. All hypotheses are admissible; but categorical conclusions would still be impertinent.

Even such as it is now, incomplete and developing, leftist theory represents a confluence of several disparate influences. Its aims of radical transformation are inherited from Marxism, yet it conceives radicalism differently and in a broader sense. It accepts the Marxist idea of the class struggle, but includes in its notion of class all who do not have control over their own destinies and the ordering of whose activities does not lie in their own hands. It thus greatly enlarges the range of alienations weighing upon the individual, and breaks with Marxist economic thought. It thus widens the 'battleground' by refusing to restrict it to the framework of the workplace. It carries the battle into the very heart of everyday life. It insinuates it into every level of existence – for leftism perceives repression at every level.

In fact, the *whole* of existence is called in question, simultaneously. Leftism considers that man is alienated in his sexual life because his real desires are stifled from infancy by morality, the family, the school. He is socialized by the patriarchal family which reproduces the authoritarian model of world society; the child is already trained to obey without question, to accept the fundamental division between those who command and those who do as they are told. The whole concept of education and discipline is such as to compel the child to inhibit his instincts of creativity and independence. The university, finally, transmits an ideological form of knowledge, and there is no academic discipline, not even the exact sciences, which in the end does not result in manipulating the student, in imposing on him a view of society, of happiness and of freedom, which is merely the reflection of a structure of domination. Having served a long apprenticeship of submission, man finds himself caught in a dense network of reifications and his consciousness is clouded by mystique. This explains the great difficulty he experiences in organizing his own authentic liberation; it explains why he is such a poor judge of his own interests and why he never ceases to wander from one kind of slavery to another. Until now, he has never been able to do more than exchange one master for another.

Now it has become a question of getting rid of all masters and all the shackles that impede our liberty. Here again, leftism dissociates itself from Marxism and from all the varieties of nineteenth-century socialism. It rejects productive labour, hoping to replace it by free, playtime activity, to which art is the closest existing approximation. It therefore dissociates itself from the mentality of the industrial society that first imposed itself in Europe at the dawn of the capitalist era. It has inherited from the dadaist and surrealist tradition a supreme contempt for the technological society, its greyness and boredom. From millenarianism and the 'horsemen of the Apocalypse' it has borrowed the aspiration towards a totally different world, a paradise which can and should be realized on earth without delay. It takes its fantastic constructions from utopia, but wants to integrate them into its short-term projects; it refuses to banish the dream and boil down the real to what is currently achievable. Finally, it aspires to build a life in which man is not a stranger to his fellows, where communication can be restored through a de-alienated use of language. The word will then be inseparable from the deed and will express human and universal truth and not squalid everyday lies.

The struggle for a new world cannot use the reified instruments of the opposition movement inherited from the past. The irruption of subjectivity into everyday claims makes reconciliation with the principle of revolutionary leadership impossible: the right to the autonomy of struggle is the first victory of the conscious revolutionary. To be *conscious* means to be master of his own destiny. His consciousness results precisely from his situation in the historical process taking place around him: it cannot be injected, increased, reinforced or initiated by any *deus ex machina*.

Leftism believes it has found in our period of history, the period now beginning, the moment when the objective situation will finally allow subjectivity to assert itself. This situation results from the emergence, in a few privileged countries, of relative affluence which encourages man to withdraw his attention somewhat from the struggle for basic survival. This 'availability', previously unknown, leads him to ask questions about the existing order of things; he can become aware, if dimly, of the extension of the realm of the possible and the tangible. It is this conscious awareness of a realizable but forbidden future which contains the energy which will enable the proletarian to tear himself away from the burden of the condition to which he was born. He will then find buried deep inside himself miracles of intelligence, infinite potentialities and, above all, an unsuspected appetite for the creation of his own destiny.

These aspirations and these energies are embodied in total and general *contestation* of the existing system, of all present systems; this is the concrete translation of all his apocalyptic visions. The leftist is convinced that the development of active dissent, of what we have here termed '*contestation*', will not fail to confirm his analyses and his predictions. How slender is the thread on which such confirmation currently hangs has already been indicated. Nevertheless, the significant indicators, found simultaneously in Warsaw and in Mexico, in Paris and in Berkeley, in Turin and in Osaka, have added a new dimension and lent a certain weight to *contestation*. But how are these indicators, which bear witness to a change both qualitative and in intensity in the world's social and political struggles, to be interpreted? In a universe which tends towards the rational organization of every aspect of life, could these not be seen as the last convulsions of a world that is approaching its end? Are these not the final explosions of a century which has never ceased to reverberate to the noise of explosions? A last broadside in salute to a dying era, an anachronistic phenomenon before humanity accedes to the era of *management* where there will be no place either for contestation or for 'workers' insurrections'.

Another hypothesis claims that the generalization of total *contestation* and the features it now manifests may be seen as the signs heralding an epoch that is only just beginning, and in the course of which humanity will free itself from the last of its chains; in which art will come out of the museums and set itself up in the street. *Contestation* as it has been witnessed over the last few years is merely a prelude to more intense, radical and also more conscious struggles.

Which of these two interpretations should we choose? No doubt the objection will be raised that both are false, because both are extreme; that the inevitable middle course will be the eventual solution. That is possible. What remains true is that leftist theory will only acquire its full meaning or its true dimension in the future: only the future can tell if its pretension to renew the theory of revolutionary movements is justified. Even so, its enormous ambitions make it worthy of study.

For the time being, we can only observe that ideas thrown out at random, and actions which were hardly intended to be seen as 'examples', have found an unexpected response. Leftism has elevated itself from Byzantine ratiocinations to the level of a doctrine: its few exponents have been replaced by numerous groups, even by unorganized masses who have adopted the same attitudes, and follow the same reasoning. The marginal sects of yesterday have taken on the impetus of a social movement.

Without prejudging its future, it may already be said that its immediacy is due to the tremendous changes which have taken place in the everyday lives of millions of individuals in so-called affluent societies. A whole realm of existence has been transformed for the working class with the increase in real income, and the guarantees created against the principal risks of working and family life with the disappearance of endemic unemployment.

Technological and scientific progress has indubitably assured a mastery of nature that was inconceivable even a quarter of a century ago. While the material conditions of everyday life have been improving, new ambitions began to surface from the depth of the human consciousness. In these circumstances leftism may be regarded as having provided original answers to new questions. It sees itself as providing no less than the promise of a predictable future. Its success depends, without doubt, on the rightness of those answers and the validity of that promise. But even now, as yet simple and incomplete, it represents a major effort of imagination in a world which seemed to be devoid of it.

This lack of imagination is peculiarly characteristic of what has generally been accepted as the left. And first in this category is official communism, the 'legitimate' heir to the revolutionary tradition of almost two centuries of social struggle. Leftism has made irreversible inroads into this monopoly. Whether leftism will become *the* revolutionary movement is an open question; but it has certainly demonstrated by its very existence and by the echo it has aroused, that this mantle is no longer worn by organized Marxism–Leninism.

Index